I would like to dedicate this work to my two children, François-Charles and Marie-Hélène and to everyone of their generation, in the hope that our efforts in building a better society will constitute a heritage on which we all can grow.

C.S.

To my colleagues and friends, who share the view that informed and enlightened public policy is a crucial part of building the information future.

C.E.F.

Founded in 1972, the Institute for Research on Public Policy is an independent, national, non-profit organization. Its mission is to improve public policy in Canada by promoting and contributing to a policy process that is more broadly based, informed and effective.

In pursuit of this mission, the IRPP

- identifies significant public policy questions that will confront Canada in the longer term future and undertakes independent research into these questions;

- promotes wide dissemination of key results from its own and other research activities;

- encourages non-partisan discussion and criticism of public policy issues in a manner which elicits broad participation from all sectors and regions of Canadian society and links research with processes of social learning and policy formation.

The IRPP's independence is assured by an endowment fund, to which federal and provincial governments and the private sector have contributed.

Créé en 1972, l'Institut de recherche en politiques publiques est un organisme national et indépendant à but non lucratif.

L'IRPP a pour mission de favoriser le développement de la pensée politique au Canada par son appui et son apport à un processus élargi, plus éclairé et plus efficace d'élaboration et d'expression des politiques publiques.

Dans le cadre de cette mission, l'IRPP a pour mandat :

- d'identifier les questions politiques auxquelles le Canada sera confronté dans l'avenir et d'entreprendre des recherches indépendantes à leur sujet;

- de favoriser une large diffusion des résultats les plus importants de ses propres recherches et de celles des autres sur ces questions;

- de promouvoir une analyse et une discussion objectives des questions politiques de manière à faire participer activement au débat public tous les secteurs de la société canadienne et toutes les régions du pays, et à rattacher la recherche à l'évolution sociale et à l'élaboration de politiques.

L'indépendance de l'IRPP est assurée par les revenus d'un fonds de dotation auquel ont souscrit les gouvernements fédéral et provinciaux, ainsi que le secteur privé.

INSTITUTE FOR RESEARCH ON PUBLIC POLICY

iRPP

INSTITUT DE RECHERCHE EN POLITIQUES PUBLIQUES

THE
MEDIUM
AND THE
MUSE

CULTURE, TELECOMMUNICATIONS AND THE INFORMATION HIGHWAY

by Charles Sirois and Claude E. Forget

IRPP

Bibliothèque nationale du Québec
Dépôt légal 1995

Canadian Cataloguing in Publication Data

Forget, Claude E., 1936-
The medium and the muse : culture, telecommunications and the information highway

Includes bibliographical references

ISBN 0-88645-175-2

1. Information networks—Canada.
2. Computer networks—Canada. 3. Telecommunication—Economic aspects—Canada.
4. Telecommunication—Social aspects—Canada.
I. Sirois, Charles II. Institute for Research on Public Policy. III. Title.

HC120.I55F67 1995   384.3'0971   C95-900115-8

Marye Ménard-Bos
Director of Publications, IRPP

Copy Editing
Mathew Horsman

Design and Production
Ric Little and Barbara Rosenstein

Cover Illustration
Tanya Johnston

Published by
The Institute for Research on Public Policy (IRPP)
L'Institut de recherche en politiques publiques
1470 Peel Street, Suite 200
Montreal, Quebec H3A 1T1

Distributed by
Renouf Publishing Co. Ltd.
1294 Algoma Road
Ottawa, Ontario K1B 3W8
Tel. 613-741-4333
Fax 613-741-5439

CONTENTS

LIST OF CHARTS AND FIGURES

FOREWORD

The decision to produce this essay was made during one afternoon in October 1994, following the latest in a series of brainstorming sessions dedicated to developing, reviewing and challenging the key strategies that our governments and enterprises should adopt if we are to fully benefit from the profound and permanent changes created by the Information Highway. These sessions had been going on for a period of eight months.

One of us had long contemplated setting down a vision of the structure and evolution of the telecommunications industry in Canada. The trigger that prompted the following pages was our work in connection with the Advisory Council on the Information Highway and more recently the Order in Council mandating a CRTC consultation. In order to position Canada at the vanguard of change, we believe that current official policies must be changed to take fully into account special opportunities and challenges that have particular relevance to Canada.

This essay does not claim to offer comprehensive solutions. We hope, instead, to offer a framework for all Canadians driven by the desire to contribute to building our future. We have undertaken this project as Canadian citizens; it does not reflect, therefore, any corporate or institutional view.

It would have been impossible to execute this work in such a short period of time without the collaboration and commitment of many people. We would like to thank Carole Deniger of Groupe Secor for her help in providing data and information on cultural industries that we found invaluable in writing chapters 3 and 4. Denis Akzam of Teleglobe Canada provided valuable information, documentation and comments with regard to telecommunications and, in particular, the interplay between technology and public policy.

We are grateful to Mathew Horsman of the Institute for Research on Public Policy for impeccable copy editing and his welcome suggestion for the title. Without the commitment of IRPP Director of Publications Marye Ménard-Bos, who supervised the physical production of this book, our tight deadlines could not have been met. Diane Lacroix produced innumerable versions of the manuscript at a gruelling pace and without losing her usual enthusiasm.

The remaining omissions, errors and blind spots are entirely our responsibility and, we would like to believe, these would have been less numerous had we devoted more than the fifty days that elapsed between start and finish.

Charles Sirois
Claude E. Forget
Montréal, December 9, 1994

ONE

INTRODUCTION

The Information Highway (I-Way) holds out the promise of lower prices for a vast variety of services and the prospect of intriguing new products and services. These tangible benefits, coupled with the universal fascination with technology, make the whole concept of the I-Way appear extremely seductive. The promise of more and better products and services, at more affordable prices, is almost too good to be true. Yet it is not merely empty rhetoric. Fibre optics and computers have already delivered on the promise in the field of telecommunications; and it is relatively easy to believe that, when everything that we now know to be technologically feasible becomes a reality, the I-Way will have launched a new-wave industrial revolution.

The contours of that revolution are already visible, and the process has been hastened by the decreasing cost of long distance telecommunications, the expansion of distance-learning opportunities and the introduction of more accessible public services. Highly specialized medical care available through remote diagnostic and therapeutic procedures, video and interactive games available on demand, more and more data on any given subject and more easily retrievable, personalized wireless communications networks that follow the consumer wherever she or he may be – these and other emerging possibilities create a powerful argument for speeding up the construction of the I-Way, removing obstacles in its way, creating incentives to stimulate innovation and, generally speaking, making tomorrow happen today.

Political leaders in most developed countries have sensed the potential in the idea of an information highway, and have been drawn particularly to its usefulness in countering frequently grim economic and financial news from other quarters. The media have been caught up in the excitement, contributing vivid descriptions of the world to come that imply nothing short of a revolutionary change in our lifestyles, spanning learning, entertainment and business. It also seems generally assumed that this revolution will come about of its own accord if only we can dismantle in time the obstacles standing in its way. Public debate focusses on the work of removing obstacles; it is a debate, therefore, about means and not ends.

The chief means suggested are greater competition, deregulation and, in some countries, privatization. Such policies have indeed already been significant in bringing about lower prices and hastening the introduction of new products and services. As a result, not only are the objectives seemingly clear but the choice of policy instruments needed to achieve the goals likewise appears obvious. The feeling that we know where we are going and know how to get there – not often prevalent when it comes to public policy making these days – has an exhilarating effect. There is no surprise in the news that many countries, including Canada, are accelerating their pace along this well-marked road.

Side considerations exist for which solutions are not so evident: the issue of privacy, universal service funding, the need to police the I-Way to prevent criminal or abusive use, the predictable desire of governments to tax the value that will be added along the I-Way. However, the present lack of answers in these areas is unlikely to slow down the pace toward construction of the highway. It is just assumed that, somehow, appropriate answers will be found.[1]

This essay is not designed to sound a sour note. The excitement and enthusiasm generated by the perception that a new frontier is being opened up constitute a precious source of motivation in the absence of which life would be duller and poorer. For each country that manoeuvres itself toward the leading edge of I-Way development, the rewards are clear: the resulting ability to attract and retain the innovating individuals and firms that fuel yet greater technological development will be a source of wealth and growth.

However, sober assessment of what all this means for Canada is called for. Technological change of such magnitude is unlikely to leave various nations' relative competitive positions untouched. Some countries will be particularly apt at maximizing the advantages flowing from the I-Way while others will see their relative positions deteriorate – even if, as might be hoped, all countries end up being better off, overall, than before. It should be remembered that relative advantage counts for a lot.

Will highway-related developments leave Canada behind in the international competitive race? Are there policy choices that Canada can make now that would enhance our ability to derive benefits down the road? What are they? The policy issues concern, essentially, the question of jobs and per-capita wealth creation. No policy, however clever, can ensure that Canada will benefit in any given set of circumstances; much more than public policy on its own determines that. However, public policy can enhance the probability of success. This is an important point that will be considered in this essay.

In order to determine effective public policy in this domain, it is necessary to consider Canada's present competitive position and performance and to make a careful assessment of two major challenges facing the country — namely, infrastructure development and cultural policy.

From a global perspective, Canada ranks very well in terms of what has been called the "telecompetitiveness" index.[2] It has a highly developed infrastructure, efficient services, a regulatory environment that, in light of current events, must be considered among the most favourable and an industrial structure in the telecommunications industry judged by some as the most appropriate in this rapidly evolving environment. It has an equipment manufacturing industry that is globally competitive and export-oriented and a telecommunications industry that contributes more than its share to the total value added in that sector among developed economies. Will the revolutionary changes in prospect enhance or undermine these advantages? With the shifting emphasis from infrastructure to services and from hardware to software, will the Achilles' heel of Canada turn out to be its huge territory and small population, characteristics that quickly become a problem in industry after industry where infrastructure spending is a significant factor?

Both the Canadian railway and airline industries face unique challenges because of Canada's low population density along most routes. In the telecommunications industry, this difficulty is compounded. Traffic on the I-Way travels at the speed of light and, with fibre-optic technology, the marginal cost implications of distance are rapidly falling toward zero. As this happens, it is already a fact that the largest population centres in Canada, almost all of them situated within a thin three-hundred kilometre strip along the Canada/US border, could have all their long distance telecommunications needs served at a lesser cost *via* the US. The end-user would not see the difference that would result from such a bypassing of Canadian infrastructure; however, soon enough, the Canadian industry would no longer be able to pay its way. The resulting increment in US long distance traffic, on the order of about 11 percent, would be hardly noticeable and is well within the excess capacity available on existing links. This fact, added to the erosion of the principle of public carriage,[3] could rapidly result in a fatal undermining of the viability of companies operating Canadian infrastructure facilities, thereby threatening their ability to provide universal service. Whatever policy is defined to meet the challenges, it will need to incorporate measures to optimize the use of resources allocated to infrastructure development. When the very viability of Canadian operations is at stake, the need to avoid building duplicate facilities should be self-evident.

No other country finds itself faced with Canada's characteristics: the huge demographic differences between it and its key neighbour; its very low population and hence low traffic density; and a distribution pattern of economic activity concentrated on a thin strip along the 5,000-kilometre border it shares with the US. Because of this unique set of circumstances, Canadians must be wary of adopting policy orientations developed elsewhere in very different contexts. However, this is not the only way in which Canada's proximity to the US is relevant. The ability to digitize all signals and the adoption of flexible service independent platforms together give rise to the possibility of using the same networks to carry different bandwidth applications – in other words, to carry not only voice conversations but also data and video programs.

Digitization, Bandwidth and Asynchronous Transfer Mode

Any image or sound, when sent or received via telephone, fax machine, or television cable, is transformed into electromagnetic impulses or "signals." The signals are said to be digital when these impulses take the form of a series of "on" and "off" values. The more complex the signals (for instance a colour picture in motion is more complex than a simple conversation), the more such impulses are needed per unit of time; therefore, the conduit needs to be wider to allow for their simultaneous passage. Hence, the distinction between narrow and broad bandwidth. It used to be difficult to carry signals at different bandwidths over the same circuit; however, with the development of asynchronous transfer mode (ATM), a method to package signals into a standardized format or "cell" (whatever their original bandwidth), all types of signals can simultaneously use the same carriage infrastructure. In this new technology, designed with multimedia in mind, the technological functions needed to manage the network can be distinguished from those needed to route individual cells through the network and can be linked to other service management software. The core elements – the physical transfer medium (such as fibre optic cable) and the lower-order switching functions – can therefore become a "service independent platform."

This is the precondition for the much-discussed "convergence" of the telecommunications and the broadcasting sectors. In many countries, this is seen as just another interesting implication of emerging technological change, contributing to the attractiveness of the I-Way and providing merely one additional reason to speed up construction. However, in Canada convergence creates an apparent policy dilemma. With regard to telecommunications, the advantages of the I-Way are incontrovertible and therefore help propel Canadian policy in the direction of ensuring an openly competitive environment to achieve the objectives of cheaper and better telecommunications. However, when it comes to broadcasting, and all other elements of content generation, the tendency is instead to fear the impact the I-Way might have on very important pillars of Canada's cultural policy and to believe as a consequence that an open, competitive environment would precipitate the Americanization of Canada.

In this essay, we certainly recognize two legitimate concerns: first, that Canadians should be able to express their own identity and see themselves reflected through the I-Way; and second, that they should be able to participate in the global I-Way as creators, service providers and carriers, not just as consumers. The promises of the I-Way are worth nothing if they are not consistent with the promotion of true diversity. The goal is not to keep American-generated content out of Canada but to ensure that the wonders of technology are effectively used to expand our horizons, making the full spectrum of human interests, outlooks and creativity accessible to all, with as little bias as possible, in an open environment – while at the same time creating wealth and prosperity for Canadians. There should be room for the expression of Canadian talent and the exercise of Canadian entrepreneurship not just in Canada but in the US and elsewhere. The question is: paying due attention to economic realities and the relatively small size of Canada and its proximity to the US, how can such an open environment be fostered?

Until now, Canada's cultural identity has been protected by such measures as outright grants to national and provincial institutions, a quota-based policy to "create" a market for Canadian music recordings and programming and a system of subsidies and tax incentives for film production. These policies have been effective and have created momentum in favour of their continued use in the service of protecting culture. The advent of new technologies, which constitute a fresh threat to Canada's achievements in the cultural sphere, is provoking a natural reaction: a desire to extend these same protective measures to the I-Way. At the time of writing, this desire is fuelling debate over the rules that ought to apply to the distribution of video signals by satellites directly to homes. Holding to our traditional approach implies further restrictions on the use of I-Way licences in Canada, a search for ways of extending cultural exemptions in trade agreements to cover new applications or, indeed, the development of alternative policies to deal with the new environment of the I-Way.

Here, then, is the apparent dilemma. For telecommunications, the policies most frequently advocated to further Canada's competitive position entail encouraging even greater reliance on competition and deregulation. For broadcasting, by contrast, the most frequently mentioned policies seem to suggest not competition but protectionism. Is this polarization really required?

This essay contains suggestions on how Canada ought to address the challenges posed by the emergence of the I-Way. More specifically, it will be argued that there is, in fact, a surprising degree of *congruence* among three sets of policy measures: first, those aimed at helping the country maximize its advantages with regard to telecommunications in the global setting; second, those focussed on building and maintaining a viable infrastructure for everyone in Canada; and third, those designed to help Canada achieve success with regard to content production and broadcasting.

However, as we will attempt to show, if effective policy regarding the I-Way is to be developed to regulate infrastructure use and content production, we must engineer a dramatic shift in existing strategies. More and more, a reassessment of policy involves taking into account the international context within which this great competitive game will be played by all countries, including Canada, and within which success or failure will increasingly be defined.

Notes

1. For a considered discussion of some of these issues, see the Honourable Justice John Sopinka, "Freedom of Speech and Privacy in the Information Age," an address presented at the University of Waterloo Symposium on Free Speech and Privacy in the Information Age, November 26, 1994, mimeo.

2. William H. Davidson and Ronald D. Hubert, "Telecompetitiveness Infostructure," a Mesa Research project sponsored by Northern Telecom (May 1994; unpublished). See also, Ronald D. Hubert, "An Analysis of Competitive Regulatory and Policy Structures based on the Telecompetitiveness Index," Proceedings of the IRPP Conference on the New Economics of Telecommunications (forthcoming).

3. Eli M. Noam, "Beyond Liberalization II: The Impending Doom of Common Carriage," *Telecommunications Policy,* Vol. 18, no. 6 (July 1994), pp. 435-52. Noam argues that the growth of private lines and other contract services is inexorably shrinking the domain left for common carriage, which suffers from an incurable competitive disadvantage. This development has ominous consequences for the viability of open systems and even for free speech.

TWO

THE INFORMATION HIGHWAY
AS AN OPPORTUNITY

The promise held out by the I-Way is truly dazzling. While much of that promise will only be realized in the future, the contours of the revolution are evident today.

Some of the more breathless descriptions of the I-Way's implications appear designed to make us believe it will trigger a new form of civilization: that it will become an essential condition for community development and an indispensable ingredient of personal success and economic growth. If we believe such descriptions, we might expect to see the emergence of new cleavages in the world, no longer so much among countries, on the basis of average per-capita income, but among groups of people at regional or sub-regional level, on the basis of whether or not they have effective access to the I-Way.

Within developed countries, regional disparities in economic growth and employment opportunities could potentially be erased: the I-Way could make distance from urban centres irrelevant as a cause of relative regional underdevelopment. For those of our generation, it is easy to believe that technology can indeed trigger such profound changes, since it has already done so several times in our lifetime. History teaches us that the same is true of the 19th century as well. For some people, however, even this contention is not sufficiently dramatic. Enthusiasts will tell us the revolution ushered in by the I-Way is of similar magnitude to the industrial revolution that transformed the world over the course of the late 18th and early 19th centuries, constituting one of the very few monumental discontinuities in human history.[1] The industrial revolution initiated the gradual replacement of human and animal muscle power by machines, whereas the ongoing computer and telecommunications revolution augments and in some cases (e.g., with regard to memory) supplants the human brain.

The I-Way: Reasons for Scepticism

Such assertions concerning the extent of the revolution remain controversial. It is relatively easy to point to the absence of hard evidence regarding demand for many of the anticipated products and services that will be carried on the I-Way. In the best of circumstances, it takes a long time to generate effective demand for totally new products. Recent technological breakthroughs that are now widely in use around the world, such as automatic teller machines for banks or the now ubiquitous fax machine, were around 10 to 15 years before they really caught on. The ROM disc, on the market since 1986, is only now beginning to be widely used.

In effect, these technologies were initially not perceived as offering any-thing really new — anything, that is, that human bank tellers, postal and courier services or, say, directories and encyclopedias, did not already offer, except of course convenience, 24-hour availability and speed. Indeed, it is these attributes rather than the services themselves that represent the true innovation: and such innovation could only really be appreciated after peo-ple had a chance to experience the new services for some time. By that time there was no going back to the old ways, and the industries built up around these technological innovations appear solid indeed.

Doubts about the early success of the I-Way can be justified in other ways as well. For instance, it is common knowledge that the user-friendly software needed to access all products and services promised by the I-Way has not yet been adequately developed. Entertaining stories about the inability of even well-educated and reasonably sophisticated consumers to program their video recorders in order to "time-shift" television programs are legion. The current lack of easy-to-use, transparent and efficient content retrieval equip-ment and software remains a significant bottleneck on the I-Way, although this is gradually being remedied — at least for the Internet, if not yet for the full-fledged I-Way.[2] Projects to develop better access software, involving Microsoft, IBM and a host of other software houses grouped under a number of strategic alliances, have been well publicized but have yet to bear fruit.

As well, given the industrial organization in place in most countries, inno-vation still depends to a significant extent on the decisions taken by firms already active in the fields where the I-Way will one day compete. If the I-Way turns out to be as successful as anticipated, it will have a massive displacement effect on the services already provided by existing players. The temptation to depreciate existing assets more fully before introducing innovative substitute services may therefore slow down the pace of change.

On this point, consider an instructive example. There has been for years speculation that traditional telephones would give way to videophones, which allow callers and respondents to see each other. It seems clear that this cannot happen without replacing the traditional technology embodied in the pair of twisted copper wires installed in each home. There would be no other use for these wires – they constitute what is termed a "sunk cost." Given that telephone companies switching to new technology for the purpose of providing video telephony would have to abandon copper wiring, they would have to write off these undepreciated assets at the time they made the decision. This would be painful enough on its own, but would in addition threaten their ability to finance the installation of replacement technology. Moreover, if a competitor (by definition not itself a "traditional" telephone company) also provided the new technology, it could expect vigourous price-cutting by the telephone company, since any price that allowed the telephone company to cover at least part of the depreciation charge (in addition to operating costs) would be preferable to total defeat.

Finally, there is a useful distinction to be made between, on the one hand, the I-Way as a transmission vehicle for existing products and services such as films, sport events, news, public affairs, dramatic series, video games, video conferencing, CD-ROM-based, encyclopedia-like databases and, on the other, as a medium for interactive programs and transaction-oriented services. Almost all the anticipated passive (i.e., non-interactive) content that will be carried by the I-Way already exists and is now carried by other media. In this context, then, the promise of the I-Way is merely to provide greater convenience, less costly carriage and better quality. These attributes are very important and may make a great difference. But are they truly radical?

All these reasons for scepticism aside, it is conceivable that the highway will spawn yet-to-be-developed products and services that we cannot even imagine at present. Let us bear in mind that technologies that are now taken for granted such as the cinema, radio broadcasting, music recording and television all resulted in totally new products that were previously unthinkable. Even futurologists have difficulty hinting at what these totally new products and services might be, with the exception, of course, of virtual reality.[3]

We assume that resistance to what is new and unfamiliar will be overcome; that user-friendly equipment and software will be developed; that the I-Way will add attributes to "old" content that will be appreciated and generate demand; that entirely new products and services – including interactive ones – will emerge; that, finally, the deadweight of sunk capital will work itself out or be overcome. In other words, we believe that change is inevitable and can at most be briefly delayed. Debates about whether or not this is so are frankly a waste of time: we would be better off preparing ourselves to adapt to change.

Given these assumptions, we also venture to suggest that the general characteristics of the I-Way (whether or not new or existing products and services are involved) as well as those characteristics that represent the sharpest break with the past, can be inferred today from the nature of the technology.

Immediacy, Consumer Choice and Low Costs

The most obvious consequences of the huge leap in capacity made possible by the new technologies will be the elimination of distance as a factor in telecommunications and the availability of broad bandwidth. The transformation of telecom carrying capacity into a mundane "commodity" bought and sold on the basis of lower and lower prices is virtually certain to occur, given both the scramble to build new connections and the boosts to capacity represented by ATM switching multiplexing and compression techniques.

Multiplexing, voice and video compression

Multiplexing, voice and video compression are all methods to trick telecom carriage channels (such as a telephone copper wire, a coaxial cable or a fibre optic cable) to bear traffic that, without such methods, would be beyond the capacity of the channels. These methods are embodied in machines like coder/decoders (CODEC) or multiplexers that are, in effect, special-purpose computers.

For instance, for a video signal to be of ideal "broadcast quality" it should be transmitted at 90 million "bits" (0/1 or "on/off") per second (this is written as 90 Mbps). However if one is willing to sacrifice quality and does not mind slow-moving images, the same video signal can be carried by transmitting only 56,000 bits per second (written as 56 Kbps) – i.e., only 0.06 percent as much! That might be acceptable, say, for a video conference.

In addition, video compression relies in part on comparing successive "frames" being transmitted and only transmitting those parts that would be perceived as being different; the unchanged frames would simply be repeated at the receiving end.

The principles of voice compression and video compression are varied and subject to ongoing improvements. These methods involve technical sophistication beyond the scope of this essay. However, an intuitive understanding is possible by considering a common enough question asked about voice multiplexing and/or compression, namely, how is it that five simultaneous conversations can be carried on a single circuit and not become hopelessly jumbled? One answer can be found by reference to a very imperfect analogy: no one would confuse the sounds of a piano playing, a dog barking and a telephone ringing heard simultaneously in the same room!

The result would be to create "one world" more effectively than jet aircraft technology ever could. This impact would occur across the entire spectrum of frequencies or bandwidth but, naturally, its effect would be greater in absolute terms at broader bandwidth. This is because user charges reflect not only distance but also bandwidth. The price reductions for video conferencing, for example, are so substantial that a threshold level is quickly reached, leading to a big increase in use.

The vision of the entire planet becoming a "global village" must be tempered by reality. Only countries, regions, cities and groups with access to the I-Way will be affected. Consistent with the economics of an industry with high fixed costs related to infrastructure but with potentially very low costs for high-volume usage, the I-Way will either be very inexpensive or unaffordable. No community larger than a yet-to-be-determined threshold size and with moderate average income need ever be "remote" in the telecommunications sense; however, if these conditions are not met, the sense of isolation may be relatively worse than now. This raises obvious policy questions.

Virtually limitless carriage capacity, combined with ever-expanding computer applications for switching, data bank management and information retrieval means that a second major characteristic of the I-Way consists in dramatically expanded *consumer choice,* which in turn will change the economics of the creation and distribution of content. This expanded choice will provide an illustration of Schumpeter's principle of creative destruction.[4]

Virtually limitless choice will destroy most of the remaining economic rents.[5] Until the advent of cable transmission and satellite television, mass media economics, and especially TV economics, was characterized by rationing. This is because spectrum limitations affecting ground-based, off-air broadcasting (as opposed to satellite broadcasting) generated high situation rents for a small number of large networks. These rents were a well-known phenomenon in North America; elsewhere, where state monopolies in television broadcasting were erected, they did not arise. The North American system made possible large profits but also gave the television chain owners considerable power *vis-à-vis* content producers and consumers. The situation rents were subjected to gradual erosion by cable and satellite television, as evidenced in the US by the decline in the audience shares of the major TV networks, a phenomenon also experienced in Canada and other countries. In terms of market penetration, cable television and Direct Broadcast Satellites (DBS) are still relatively recent developments in most countries.

Even in the US, satellite TV only accounts for a minuscule share of the total market. The 500-channel world – a metaphor for unlimited access to video content, driven by consumer choice – will eventually complete the dismantling of these rent-yielding situations. With the multiplication of alternative technologies to carry video signals, there is no reason why these rents should be re-established. They belong as firmly to the past as the steam engine.

In other words, value was created in the past through the ownership and use of scarce infrastructure: scarce because the available electro-magnetic spectrum is limited. Value will now emerge from meeting the demands of end-users. What fails to satisfy that demand will have no value because end-users will be free to turn to other offerings. In the value chain, everyone from the manufacturer of equipment and the film producer to the facilities operator and the service providers adds a portion of the total ultimate value of the content chosen by end-users. The I-Way shifts the "place" where value is added, pushing it closer to the consumers and further away from the infrastructure.

The I-Way: A Major Break With the Past

To sum up, consumer choice, affordable access to broad bandwidth and the elimination of distance as an economic factor in telecommunications are key characteristics of the I-Way: if creatively exploited, they will determine the success of individual products and service offerings. These characteristics also mark the unique contribution of the I-Way to a different lifestyle – indeed, a new form of civilization or at least of social organization. To learn to put these features to work in the design of new products and the development of new businesses is at the same time to challenge content packagers. That challenge is addressed quite specifically at content packagers as opposed to equipment makers or communications carriers or even content producers as such. For it is the packagers who will make of the I-Way a source of a major discontinuity in the development of broadcasting, telecommunications services and associated activities. It is here, in other words, that a break can happen, triggering a series of dramatic consequences for established players.[6]

Consider an historical analogy. When the film industry emerged in the 1920s to exploit the new technology of the cinema, major film production companies were established not in New York or in London where theatre production in English was thriving but rather in what was then, relatively speaking, the wilderness of Hollywood, where an abundance of natural sunlight (and as yet no smog) was the most significant asset. Theatre owners did not become film producers for much the same reason that the Western Union Telegraph Company did not become a major telephone company. Western Union was, at the beginning of the 20th century, the dominant force in telecommunications, holding an unassailable position in telegraph services. It ignored the potential of the telephone, which it would have been well positioned to exploit, in part because of its own sunk costs in telegraph facilities and in part because it firmly believed that the public would always prefer the written confirmation that the telegraph (but not the telephone) provided! The significance of major discontinuities is that they make it likely that the cards will be reshuffled and distributed according to a completely new pattern. If that reshuffling can be seen as an opportunity, it can be the basis for strategic advantages. In any field, the largest opportunities arise in such periods of discontinuity.

Are such opportunities arising now? As we described earlier, timing is a major source of uncertainty with regard to the I-Way. The success of the Internet is sometimes offered as an indication that the whole world is ready to jump onto the I-Way and that this urge is only stifled by the slowness of policy makers and investors. The success of Internet, though of undoubted interest, is a misleading indicator. The Internet relies on existing and even obsolescent technology, not on the new technology promised by the I-Way. In its present form, it is heavily dependent on US government subsidies; by its very nature, it is something of a high-tech toy that is bound to attract a circumscribed group of *aficionados* who, though numerous, account for a very small part of the total population.

While it is true that the I-Way still has many hurdles to overcome and that there is still time for careful planning, it would nonetheless be unwise to proceed too slowly. One should not ignore the potential for achieving breakthroughs that will allow us to overcome the various hurdles. At the same time, we would be ill advised to overlook the ongoing, innovative work of technologists and investors, as they attempt to speed up the arrival of a new age in communications.

Change is first and foremost driven by the evolution of the telecommunications industry, characterized by the following developments: the arrival of broad bandwidth capacity; network connectivity; competitive provision of services leading to lower prices; the attention paid by powerful software production firms to the development of end-user terminal equipment and software; and the presence of entrepreneurs eager to carve out an early market presence in transactional services. The latter, in particular, may well prove to be the engine of growth, at least at the outset, enabling the industry to pay for the construction of the I-Way. Will an I-Way born of efforts to supply remote data processing, video conferencing and home shopping be capable of triggering a cultural revolution? We suggest that it is important to make sure that it is!

What Role Should Government Play?

Governments everywhere are heavily indebted and struggling with deficits. In many countries, they are privatizing telecommunications monopolies; and everywhere, they proclaim their reliance on the private sector to build and operate the I-Way. In any event, so much is happening that there is little doubt the private sector will produce something.

The current reluctance of governments to involve themselves beyond establishing broad policy directions is remarkable considering the very important, indeed leading, role that governments played when other major infrastructure was constructed. Canals and railways in the 19th century were the products of state intervention even in the US. Air travel similarly developed as a result of very substantial public investments in airports and related services, as well as in development work for airframes and engines initially undertaken for military purposes. Forerunners of the I-Way, such as the US Internet and France's Minitel, resulted from state initiative and public funding. Can the I-Way itself really constitute the first major revolutionary change triggered by massive capital investments that take place without state participation?

International capital markets can certainly raise huge amounts of money for highly speculative investments based on new technologies. For instance, a spurt of interest in genetic research, fuelled by the desire to finance medical applications, made possible the raising of hundreds of millions of dollars at the beginning of the 1980s, even though commercial applications only emerged 15 years later. Capital markets are therefore capable of long-term vision. And that is particularly true if the anticipated returns are very large. The problem with the I-Way is that it is based not on one technology but a series of more or less interconnected and interdependent technologies. Not all are reaching maturity at the same time and the time sequence in which they do is, to a large extent, random.

In such a context "there may be a tremendous first mover advantage in the market for high quality video production and distribution."[7] With all the uncertainties attached to how and when significant added value can be expected to be generated by the operation of the I-Way, the most readily available technology – even if, in a longer perspective, an inferior one – can play the same role in the field of telecommunications that "debased" currency plays in capital markets. Gresham's law says "that bad money drives out good money." Could it be, for instance, that satellite video services are, in effect, such a debased currency, one that could for a long time make deployment of a true I-Way uneconomic? With the cost of any transmission platform irretrievably sunk, new and potentially superior technology can only profitably compete if total costs are no more than the presumably very low marginal costs of the "inferior" technology it is designed to replace.

Choices are made sequentially, and there is no guarantee that a given sequence of choices with regard to infrastructure will lead to optimum deployment of resources. This statement suggests that "optimum deployment" can somehow be defined and agreed upon – no easy task, to be sure. However, the alternative – not to think about it, and merely to assume that everything will fall into place as it should and that, if mistakes are made, they can be spotted and corrected at an acceptable cost – is simply not a defensible position.[8]

There is, therefore, an important role to be played by policy makers in creating an environment where the distinguishing features of the I-Way can be fully developed. As we have tried to indicate in this chapter, these features consist, principally, in immediacy (i.e., the removal of the economic penalty that has been associated with distance in communications) and consumer choice. Technological options ought to be chosen with these objectives in mind. But Canadians – both as individuals and as owners and employees of firms – must also quickly learn to encourage the displacement of added value to other points along the value chain in telecommunications and broadcasting. Government can do much to signal and emphasize this shift and to encourage a form of industry organization that will facilitate responses to the current challenges. It is to this role of government that we now turn.

Notes

1. See Ithiel de sola Pool, "Technologies Without Boundaries," in E.M. Noam (ed.), *On Telecommunications in a Global Age*, (Cambridge, Mass.: Harvard University Press, 1990).

2. Various avenues for the development of user interfaces are stimulatingly discussed in Zachary M. Schrag, "Navigating Cyberspace – Maps and Agents – Different Uses of Computer Networks Call for Different Interfaces," in Gregory C. Staple (ed.), *Telegeography* (TeleGeography Inc., 1994), pp. 44-51. For a discussion of a successful commercial access to the Internet, namely the World Wide Web and Mosaic, a software program that helps users browse through Internet files, see Louise Kehoe, "Caught in the Web," *The Financial Times*, November 25, 1994.

3. The expression "virtual reality" is sometimes used – inappropriately – to refer to any kind of video imaging such as video graphics, animation or rotation of three dimensional shapes on a television screen *etc.* In reality, the term refers to an interactive, simultaneous electronic representation of a real or imaginary world where through sight, sound and even touch the user is given the impression of becoming part of what is represented.

4. Joseph Schumpeter, a renowned historian of economic concepts and theories coined the phrase to describe how, in a market economy, entrepreneurs introducing innovations may trigger the failure of established firms, in *Capitalism, Socialism and Democracy*, (New York: HarperCollins, 1983).

5. Economic rents are payments beyond normal returns on investment that accrue to the owner of a scarce resource (a piece of land at a busy intersection, a licence to do something that is suddenly in demand *etc.*) merely because it is, indeed, scarce and not because of any additional service derived from that resource, over and above the value of the service.

6. George Gilder in *Life After Television: the Coming Transformation of Media and American Life*, revised ed. (New York: W.W. Norton & Company, 1994) does not mince words when it comes to describing the destructive potential of the change brought about by the I-Way: "... one thing is clear. There will be no room for television or phones, or for companies that make them" (p. 24). "[T]elevision and telephone executives all too often seem unaware that their basic technologies are dead" (p. 11).

7. See Bruce L. Egan, *Information Super Highways: the Economics of Advanced Public Telecommunications Networks* (Boston: Artech House, 1991), pp. 157 and 173.

8. This is a point forcefully advocated by Elmer H. Hara, director of research and development for the Canadian Institute for Broadband and Information Network Technologies Inc., in a paper entitled "The Information Super-Highway, a One-Time Opportunity for Canada," Brief to the Information Highway Advisory Council, November 7, 1994. According to Hara if cable companies and telephone companies each install their own self-contained networks, "... all the multimedia services that might be offered by a single super-highway to the home and offices ...cannot be matched by a duopoly...This choice representing the compromise of vested commercial interests without the concern for the benefit of the public as a whole may limit Canada's prosperity." Much the same concern is expressed with regard to the ability of Direct Broadcast Satellite to pre-empt the market for video services to the home in such a way as to render economically unviable a more ambitious – and in the end more significant – universal broadband network.

THREE

THE INFORMATION HIGHWAY AS A CHALLENGE

It has been said that the whole world watches American sitcoms on Japanese-made television sets. While this is, of course, a vast oversimplification, it nevertheless epitomizes the fear sometimes felt in smaller countries of being frozen out of the global I-Way except as onlookers and consumers. It comes as no surprise that Japanese equipment makers and US entertainment firms see nothing wrong in their domination of the market, believing it to be a vindication of the principle that the most efficient in any field rightly prevails. Just as naturally, however, self-congratulation from the winners does little to reassure those who perceive themselves as potential losers.

Deriving the full benefits of the global I-Way depends on global liberalization. That means that every competitor, no matter what its country of domicile, would face a level playing field – that is, the ability, all other things being equal, to participate in all the various activities and services included in the concept of the I-Way. Extensive liberalization is a complicated, difficult and long process. Morever, the process will be even slower, indeed halted altogether, if the concept of the global I-Way is perceived as being a zero-sum game, where economies of scale and market power available only to a few firms from only the largest countries will sweep up everything in their path.

Two Stubborn Facts: the Diversity of Human Experience and the Institutional Biases Against It

The fear of being swamped goes beyond narrow questions of protectionism. It relates to different life outlooks, national cultures and value systems: people are what they eat and this is true both in the physical and the intellectual sense.

The pervasiveness of these differences is well illustrated by the different treatment of the 1994 Winter Olympics by various national television networks. Here was a single event of international interest carried roughly at the same time, sometimes even live when time zones allowed. The televised versions of the same event, for instance in the US and in Canada, were almost as distinct as they would have been had two entirely different events been reported. Some have said that Olympic sports is a substitute for war; and certainly every country's reporting paid attention to that particular nation's overall standing, measured in terms of medal counts. In the US version, this was compounded by the "heroic" treatment of each US medal winner, extending to profiles of his or her family and neighbourhood. Events in which Americans were unlikely to do well were simply ignored in favour of "human interest" stories shot in the US. The Canadian treatment of the Olympics, probably reflecting a small-country outlook on life, included reports on all events – even when no Canadian stood a chance of winning a medal – and interesting segments on the host country, Norway. These differences matter because they go far beyond the immediate topic. They reflect an entire perspective on the world that each country is naturally concerned to preserve and cultivate.

The question here is not whether Canadians can continue to enjoy Canadian broadcasting as well as US programs but whether in a world of expanding choice American *and Canadian* offerings stand anything like an equal chance of being seen and enjoyed, not only in Canada but on a global scale. And here the question goes beyond just the sheer physical capability of the I-Way to give us access to anything, anywhere, any time: it relates, as well, to the packaging, marketing and accessibility of those offerings from the users' perspective.

In this context, consider the following example. Many years ago, American Airlines, the highest volume airline in the world, developed a computerized ticket reservation system called SABRE. That system became so popular with travel agents that it was said that American Airlines was deriving greater profits from operating its reservation system than from its core business. The system was open to any airline that desired to use it, so as to facilitate the making of reservations by travel agents. However, SABRE was programmed to ensure that American Airlines flights appeared on the screen first in response to requests for flight schedules between two given cities. This was true even when other airlines on the system could provide more timely connections than American Airlines. Eventually, as a result of an anti-trust complaint, the programming of SABRE was modified to prevent American Airlines from using its control of the reservation system to create a bias in its favour. This proves that not only television programming but even data banks and data retrieval systems can reflect corporate (or national) bias.

With full digitization of sound, images and data, the global I-Way will in effect merge telecommunications with all the mass media cultural industries, information systems, educational and scientific material *etc.* In this convergent world of cultural products and telecommunications technology, the question – and the challenge – is in effect to understand how much true diversity the I-Way will offer. If through inadvertence or bad design the I-Way becomes an instrument by which the whole world hears the same things, sees the same images and eventually thinks the same thoughts, the global I-Way had better not be built. Civilization has advanced or regressed as true freedom of thought has itself ebbed and flowed. The burden of proving how genuine diversity of opinions and viewpoints can be encouraged rather than stifled by the I-Way rests firmly with those who promote the concept. Commercial freedom can do a lot to generate economic wealth through higher efficiency, lower prices and technological innovation. However, the impact of commercial freedom on cultural diversity, particularly on a global I-Way, is by no means clear. Indeed, if we were to hazard a guess, the impact may be distinctly unfavourable.

The Influence of Industrial Structure

What should Canada, a small country next to the giant US, do to improve the prospects for diversity? Canada certainly wants the chance to get its message across, to see Canadian-generated content and applications come onto the global I-Way. That necessarily involves making efforts to ensure that other national markets, and in particular the US market, are open and operate with as little bias as possible. To achieve this, there must be a trade policy appropriate to the global I-Way, a topic we address in a subsequent chapter. We must also reassess Canadian cultural industries' strategic planning and reorient cultural policies, as well as the instruments used to support them, so that they are no longer focussed so exclusively on the domestic Canadian market. This set of issues will be taken up in the next chapter.

Finally, but also crucial to success, is a set of policies related to industrial organization. Telecommunications and broadcasting will likely remain everywhere, well into the foreseeable future, regulated industries subjected to licensing requirements or at least to supervision of their performance by regulatory authorities. Such regulation has been in the past, and can continue to be in the future, a significant influence on the structure of highway-related firms.

The Canadian government should therefore not allow itself to forget the influence it has on the structure of the I-Way industry. This is its most significant lever in achieving the goals that naturally suggest themselves for both the "broadcasting" and the "telecommunications" parts of the I-Way sector. Roughly summarized, job creation and the "defence and illustration" of Canadian identity were the two overarching objectives suggested by the government of Canada in the official document published when the Advisory Council on the Information Highway was created.[1] Some policy instruments may appear more directly related to these objectives (for instance government subsidies for Canadian content production) but, in the end, nothing has quite the importance of structural policies.

So what should be the main features of a Canadian policy designed to shape the structure of the industry making up the I-Way sector? In our view, policy should be focussed on the following two second-order objectives:

- Favour a non-vertically integrated model of organization so as to lower barriers to entry, an approach that would maximize the chances for Canadians to focus on those niches and segments where they can profitably exploit the creativity and innovation fostered in the highly competitive environment for the production and distribution of I-Way content and applications. Such an environment would contrast very sharply with one where vertical integration allows for internally generated content to be distributed automatically via captive channels of distribution, with all the implicit protection that such a linkage entails.

- Minimize the spillover into Canada of the US model of industrial organization. The emerging preferred form of organization for the US I-Way industry appears strongly influenced by a model of vertical integration.

These thoughts on the relationship between industry structure and its degree of openness to independent suppliers is derived from a comparative analysis of the performance, in the US, of three different cultural industries —

film, television and book publishing. These three industries will be considered here as three alternative models of industrial organization.

The US Film Industry

The US film industry has established a strong presence worldwide, based on its ability to amortize very high production costs and – perhaps even more importantly – distribution costs over its large domestic market. Between 1980 and 1993, distribution costs for US "majors" in the film industry ranged from 38 percent to 47 percent of the figure for production costs.[2] The industry's ability to amortize these costs in the domestic market is enhanced through its fairly good control over the US distribution network, as well as, increasingly, those of several other countries, including Canada. In the US, all the "majors" are as involved in distribution as in film production (see "Vertical Integration in the US Film Industry," p. 26). This extends far and deep in several European countries, where the share of the national market controlled by US majors ranges as follows: 42 percent in France, 67 percent in Spain, 68 percent in Germany and 86 percent in the United Kingdom.[3] The motives behind such downstream vertical integration, from film production to distribution, are rendered easy to understand in chart 1, which underlines the relationship between the degree of control over distribution by the majors and the share of box office receipts accounted for by US films.

A recent report of the UK Monopolies and Mergers Commission concludes that film exhibition practices in that country reflected a "complex monopoly" operating against the public interest. The practices in question included exclusive exhibition arrangements with affiliated exhibitors and minimum runs of long duration (four weeks or more), which reduced the choice of films on offer. The parties involved – mostly US studios, their UK distribution subsidiaries and theatre chains they often control – have been subjected to a cease-and-desist order.[4]

chart 1

Relationship Between Control Over Distribution by the "Majors" and the Percentage of Box Office Receipts Represented by US Films

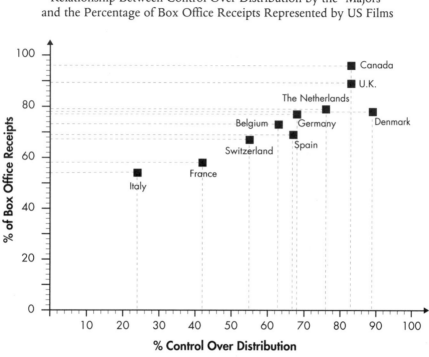

Source: *European Cinema Yearbook,* A Statistical Analysis, 1993.

Vertical Integration in the US Film Industry

- Warner Brothers and Paramount share 50-50 in the ownership of Cinamerica Theaters; through subsidiaries, Cinamerica operates 460 screens in California, Arizona, Alaska and Colorado.
- Paramount, through its parent Viacom, is linked with National Amusements Inc., operator of more than 850 cinema screens in the US and elsewhere.
- MGM wholly owns United Artists Theaters, the world's largest film exhibitor.
- Columbia owns Sony Theaters (formerly Loew's), operator of 960 screens in 180 theaters in the US.
- MCA, owner of Universal Studios, controls Cineplex-Odeon, which operates 1,065 screens in the US.

The US share of film exhibition in Canada stands at 96 percent. However, equally interesting is how the business is structured:

- The Famous Players network holds exclusive exhibition rights to first-run movies from MGM, Paramount, United Artists, Warner Brothers (English version) and Buena Vista (Disney).

- The Cineplex-Odeon chain has exclusive rights over first-run films from Columbia, Universal Pictures, Warner Brothers (French version) and Twentieth Century-Fox.

- "The Famous Players and Cineplex-Odeon chains, either formally or informally, are committed to screen not only Hollywood blockbusters but also whatever else comes from their respective studios; a policy that clutters up the screens and hurts the distribution of independently produced films."[5]

- Cineplex-Odeon (567 screens in 132 cinemas in Canada) is controlled through a 36 percent voting interest by MCA Inc., which also owns Universal Studios. A 46 percent equity share held by Bronfman family interests translates into only a 23 percent voting share. Cineplex is in fact managed from Los Angeles.

- Famous Players Canada (474 screens in 120 cinemas in Canada) is a wholly owned subsidiary of Paramount.[6]

Cinema box office receipts are an important source of income for film companies, but video sales and rentals now generate about twice as much revenue. However, ownership of video stores is not as crucial because video stores are not a distribution channel where consumer choice can so easily be directed or managed. Massive exposure of a new release in hundreds of cinemas across the country or across the world, supported by publicity campaigns, helps strengthen demand for the film at an early stage of its life cycle: this is an important factor for subsequent, non-cinema sales, as can be seen in chart 3.

chart 2

Total World Sales Generated by US Films by Market

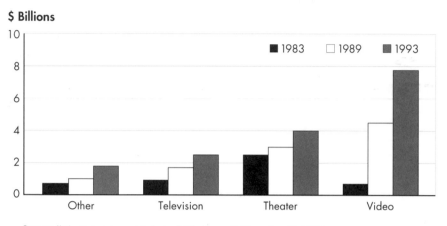

$ Billions

Source: "The Entertainment Industry," *The Economist*, December 23, 1989
(data for 1993 are forecasts)

chart 3

Life Cycle of a Popular American Film

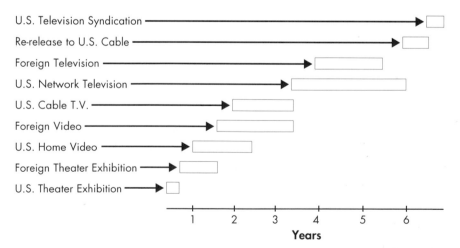

Source: "The Entertainment Industry," *The Economist*, December 23, 1989

Some of this promotional expenditure spills over into other markets, for example through the Oscar ceremony – now an event in itself, with a large non-US audience, that is useful in promoting US-style movie making. With production and promotion costs already amortized in the domestic market, the US films can then be distributed at a low marginal cost abroad – in effect "dumped," given that the foreign sales do not have carry their share of the production and promotion costs. Non-US made films enjoy very limited market presence in the US and, as a consequence, the US runs a huge balance of trade surplus with regard to film rentals and royalties. Foreign film penetration in the US market is largely limited to the "art cinemas," a niche segment that has little economic significance. Secondary markets such as cable transmission and video rentals reflect the relative absence of foreign films in movie theatres. The balance of payments picture tells an impressive tale: in 1993, US films exports to the rest of the world were worth $2,530 million while US films imports from the rest of the world were worth a mere $85 million – or only 3.32 percent of total two-way cinema trade![7]

chart 4

US 1993 Trade Flows for Film Sector*

	($ B)
Exports	2,530
Imports	85
	+ 2,445

Source: "US International Sales and Purchases of Private Services," US Department of Commerce, *Survey of Current Business,* Vol. 73 (September 1994).

* Includes transborder trade but not overseas sales by subsidiaries.

For the US film industry, vertical integration pays off handsomely but it leaves no room for non-US productions. Is this a result of consumer choice? Hardly.

The US Television Industry

The TV industry in part generates its own content but also purchases product from outside producers. It directly controls part of its infrastructure through ownership of local stations or indirectly through agreements with affiliates. In contrast to the situation in the film industry, the extent of this control by the major networks ABC, NBC and CBS has been a subject of public policy inquiries and regulation. This is not so surprising given that, unlike the film industry, broadcasting is a regulated activity.

Since the very beginning of television – that is to say from the 1950s – no fewer than three inquiries have been conducted, motivated by concern over excessive concentration in the industry. A particular target of this concern was the "option time" clause in affiliation contracts between networks and individual stations that allowed the networks to assert priority over program content and scheduling. This removed from local stations discretion over programming to reflect local preferences and also prevented competing networks or syndicated productions from gaining access to airtime. One of those inquiries (The Celler Committee) concluded that "option time was anti-competitive and inimical to the concept of freedom of choice by each station to choose the best programs available for each time period, letting each program be judged by its own merits and not through an artificial tying restraint."[8]

This condemnation of vertical integration through exclusive contractual arrangements led to a prohibition in the form of a restraint on holders of a local television licence to reach formal or informal agreements with a network along the lines of an "option time" clause.

These rules were partly circumvented when networks set up production subsidiaries to make use of the "syndication" loophole. As a result, regulation was further tightened by prohibiting syndicated productions sponsored by the networks and by limiting to three hours the length of time that network-originated programs could be shown on local stations during the four hours of prime time.

None of this prevented the three commercial television networks from dominating US airwaves for more than 20 years. The main reason resided in the limited number of channels available for television on the electro-magnetic spectrum and the high risk to a new entrant of breaking into a market where publicity revenue was highly dependent on total audience shares. When, in the late 1960s, UHF television channels were made available, the limited number of television sets that could receive the signals made market penetration a very slow process and, commercially, a non-starter.[9]

Excessive concentration in US television was a policy concern right from the start. However, given that policy makers had to fight against the inherent tendency of technology to lead to concentration, regulatory policy had only a marginal impact. This is an important lesson that should not be over-looked. The advent of cable television and video players, new technologies in both cases, began to change the situation during the 1980s. In light of the weakening grip that the major networks had on television audiences, as shown in chart 5, from over 90 percent at the end of the 1970s to 61 per-cent in 1993, policy concerns over vertical integration have lessened.

chart 5

Networks' Share of Prime Time Audience*

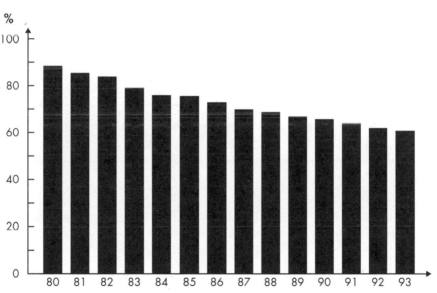

Source: "Who is watching America's TV network?", *The Economist,* March 31, 1990 for the years 1980 to 1989 and Neilsen Media Research for the years 1990 to 1993.

* Network Data includes ABC, NBC and CBS (the Fox network is excluded).

Networks are now free to broadcast their own productions and, from November 1995, they will also be allowed to enter the syndication market. Chart 6 shows that network production has been increasing since the mid-1980s and that input from both major film studios and independent producers has been declining since 1990.

chart 6

Sources of Networks' Prime Time Programming*

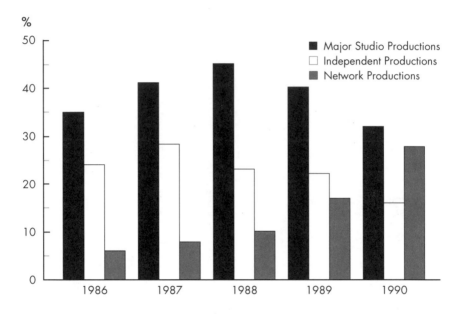

Source: Elizabeth Jensen, "Television: Where the Money Goes," *Wall Street Journal,* September 9, 1994.

* Total production is divided between the output of "majors" such as Warner Bros., Paramount, Disney *etc.*, the internal production, namely, all that is not produced by the networks or by the "majors."

Book Publishing

Book and record publishing in most countries function according to a non-vertically integrated model. Publishers use the work of independent authors, not of salaried staff or authors on contract. They use independent printers and they sell through largely independent retailers (i.e., bookstores). The US trade balance in books reflects the lesser importance of the gatekeeper function played in the other sectors by a more vertically integrated industry.

Compared to film industry imports, which are a negligible percentage of two-way flows, the book trade imports figure stands at 38.6 percent of two-way trade, as shown in chart 7.

chart 7

Trade Flows for Publishing

	($ B)
Total	
Exports	3,587
Imports	1,914
	+1,673
Periodicals	
Exports	805
Imports	167
	+ 638
Books	
Exports	1,750
Imports	1,100
	+ 650
Newspapers	
Exports	36
Imports	54
	-18

Source: US Industrial Outlook, 1993 – U.S. Department of Commerce

In the US, the book publishing industry is less concentrated than film production, with the 10 largest publishers representing 60 percent of total sales as opposed to 80 percent for the seven major film studios in their respective markets. Direct sales and tied "book of the month" clubs each represent only four percent of book sales. Bookstores are normally independent, although Disney – also a book publisher – has its own "Disney Stores," with 220 retailing locations. Simon and Schuster, the leading US book publisher, is owned (along with Prentice Hall) by Paramount, a film studio. Integration here is not only vertical but horizontal as well.

Promotion budgets of book publishers are normally modest and the campaigns are of limited scope, although spending has been increasing recently. A lot of the promotion is done at no cost to publishers as a result of book reviews, literary prizes and bestseller lists. This used to be the case for the music recording business as well, until the emergence of video clips substantially altered the economics of the industry by enhancing the importance of promotional expenses, which in turn is leading to a gradual movement toward close links between producers and distributors (record stores). This trend may result in the transformation of the music industry into something very similar to the film industry. For instance, four major labels, Warner, EMI, Polygram and Sony recently formed an alliance with Ticket Master of Los Angeles to set up a new music cable television channel that will feature the four companies' video clips and, eventually, direct sales of CDs and cassettes over a 1-800 line.

Of these three cultural industries – film, television and book publishing – two stand out as almost pure polar cases. The film industry is strongly vertically integrated and the firms making up the industry function collectively as a national cartel in the domestic and foreign markets. The publishing industry is *not* vertically integrated and has innumerable participants along with some very large firms; it is permeable to trade even if it is not entirely immune to trade-restraining practices, particularly with regard to the US-UK book trade. Neither industry is regulated.

By comparison, the US television industry represents a mixed bag. A regulated industry with very few major players, it has displayed a tendency for *de facto* vertical integration because of the very few off-air channels available and the economics of mass broadcasting: regulators were on the whole unable to effectively resist these pressures until technology, in the form of cable transmission, made the issue gradually lose relevance for policy makers, if not for the networks themselves.

As these examples show, a lesser degree of vertical integration seems associated with more true diversity in content sources, more balanced trade, and therefore less probability of cultural hegemony and a more level playing field for participants from many countries. This is an important consideration when it comes to the construction of the I-Way. It is therefore ironic, given the apparent superiority of a non-integrated model, that so many of the strategies outlined by US businesses eager to develop the I-Way appear to support the creation of fully integrated firms, with operations ranging in scope from Hollywood studios to cellular telephones.

More crucially, this is taking place at the same time as a policy vacuum is allowed to persist with regard to whether or not terminal equipment used by consumers to access the I-Way will be interconnectable and inter-operable between different service suppliers. Since the I-Way is supposed to offer choice to the consumers, there will exist a very strong temptation to slant that choice by committing the customer to one source of content and applications through terminal equipment that must be bought or leased for a long period and that incorporates proprietary technology and provider-biased access software.

Given the size of the US market and the potential for corporate behemoths, especially in the most profitable market segments, to behave as gatekeepers, excluding content that they do not originate themselves, there is a real possibility that the global I-Way that will emerge will be of far less interest than might otherwise have been the case. If the global I-Way is not about the free flow of ideas, perspectives and outlooks, what is it about? If it is not about these things, who needs it?

Implications for Canada

Canada can have no influence whatsoever on US industrial policy in the I-Way sector. The drawbacks outlined above are not so serious in a very large market such as the US, where vertically integrated giants and at least some amount of domestic competition are simultaneously possible. This, however, is not the case in Canada. And because of that, and in spite of our natural tendency to emulate American practices, the American model of vertical integration for I-Way businesses should stop at the Canadian border. This does not mean that foreign firms involved in the I-Way cannot invest in operations in Canada; however, Canadian laws should require that such foreign corporate players choose among the different hats they wear at home to decide which one they prefer to wear in Canada. This is not an unprecedented requirement either for Canada or for the US and, therefore, it should not create a major problem. Obviously, this requirement could not apply to foreign firms in Canada unless similar prohibitions existed for domestic firms.

This last point is the most important one. We have argued that vertical integration is inimical to the existence of a wide-open competitive industry of content and application producers because it creates implicit bias, high entry barriers and therefore less competition in a field where competition is the model most conducive to development and growth. If our contention is correct, then a policy reflecting this should be adopted here in Canada.

Canadian creators and content and applications producers can set for themselves very high performance goals and can be competitive on the global I-Way. This requires first that they espouse such an objective. However, it also requires that they operate in a policy environment that provides proper incentives, stimulates entrepreneurship and counteracts very forcefully any protectionist policies and business practices in Canada as well as in other countries.

Notes

1. The Canadian Information Highway: Building Canada's Information and Communications Infrastructure, *Spectrum,* Information Technologies and Telecommunications Sector, Industry Canada (April 1994).

2. Motion Picture Association of America, "US Economic Review" (Encino, CA: December 1992).

3. "European Cinema Yearbook, A Statistical Analysis, 1993," Cinema d'Europa, Media Salles (August 1993).

4. UK Monopolies and Merger Commission, "Films, A report on the supply of films for exhibition in cinemas in the UK," Department of Trade and Industry, (October 1994).

5. "L'Intégration verticale: le vrai chef d'oeuvre d'Hollywood," *Le Devoir,* December 12, 1993.

6. Much of this data comes from the annual reports of the quoted companies or their parents.

In addition see: "US International Sales and Purchases of Private Services," US Department of Commerce, *Survey of Current Business,* Vol. 73 (September 1994).

7. US Department of Commerce data.

8. The three inquiries in question are: Senate Committee on Interstate and Foreign Commerce, "The Network Monopoly," report prepared by Senator John Bricker, 84th Cong., 2nd sess. (1957); House Antitrust Subcommittee on the Judiciary, "The Television Broadcast Industry," 85th Cong. 1st sess. (1957; known as the Celler Report); House Committee on Interstate and Foreign Commerce, "Network Broadcasting," 85th Cong. 2nd sess. (1958; known as the Barrow Report).

9. Tino Balio, *Hollywood in the Age of Television* (London: Unwin Hyman, 1990).

FOUR

WILL CANADA BE THE PRISONER
OF ITS OWN SUCCESS?

The Government of Canada has long been active in promoting Canadian content in electronic mass media and cinema. This policy is carried out through a variety of means. One component resides in the decision to set up and maintain national institutions such as the National Film Board and the Canadian Broadcasting Corporation, both with a clear nation-building agenda. Another takes the form of outright financial support through organizations such as Telefilm Canada or through a regime of tax writeoffs for investments in films made in Canada. Finally, "structural measures" were developed to supplement the other means by requiring the airing of Canadian content on radio and television airwaves. These requirements have become conditions for the granting and the renewal of radio and television licences. They were later extended to the cable industry and supplemented with rules such as simultaneous substitution and the imposition of a Canadian production levy.

Cultural Protection: A Legitimate Concern

There is no doubt that there is a substantial measure of popular support for a policy designed to create a market for Canadian creative and performing talent. The need for a small country such as Canada, living next door to the US, to have a policy of actively promoting a distinct national point of view is widely accepted and has even generated a measure of support for the concept in other countries, notably in Europe.[1] As well, these various measures have met with some success, to judge by the existence of a Canadian music recording industry featuring Canadian composers and performers and a Canadian film and television production industry of some considerable magnitude, responsible for some world-class productions. Achieving and even exceeding content requirements have traditionally been easier in French language media than in English language ones for readily understandable reasons. From 1987 to 1992, foreign programs represented between 36 percent and 38 percent of television viewing time by francophones and between 73 percent and 75 percent for anglophones.[2] Over the years since implementation, these policies have generated considerable constituencies among industry proprietors and, particularly, among creative artists, producers and performers.

The national policy in question deservedly enjoys support. Indeed, it is almost impossible to find in Canada a dissenting voice about the *objectives* being pursued by the Broadcasting Act and related measures. Canadians are convinced that the world in which they live would be poorer without such a policy. This is because it has produced diversity that would probably not exist otherwise. However, the perceived success of the policy as well as the virtual unanimity about the objectives pursued contain the seed of a danger. That danger lies in the temptation for Canadians to be prisoners of their own success and of the existing consensus, while the world is changing – and profoundly – all around them. This change makes it urgent to carefully distinguish between the objectives of the policy and the practical measures taken to implement it. It is imperative to be ready to assess critically each and everyone of those means, and to gauge the "success" with which each one is credited.

What Does Success Mean?

The success alleged for Canadian structural measures aimed at creating a market for Canadian content hides a measure of ambiguity. Canadian content rules apply indiscriminately to a large variety of offerings for which the practical significance of quota requirements vary widely. First, the success of any protectionist measure can differ depending on whether one can consider its initial impact on an "infant industry" and its ongoing impact once that industry has reached a degree of maturity. We have no wish to deny that quota requirements may have been critical in triggering the emergence of some forms of Canadian content. This has been done so successfully that, in some cases, a viable market has been created, along with an expectation, on the part of listeners and viewers, that similar offerings will continue to be made available by broadcasters, irrespective of whether they are required by law to do so. After all, foreign news, to take one example, is a very imperfect substitute for national news. However, national news qualifies as "Canadian content" and helps to fill the quota. It would not now ever disappear, whatever the legal requirements.

Some content qualifies as Canadian even though it includes significant foreign elements. For instance, provided a Canadian producer is involved and provides a commentator, televised football and baseball games rate as Canadian content because the relevant leagues include a few nominally Canadian teams along with a much larger number of American teams (see below).

Canadian Content Rules

- The CRTC requires that 60% of material broadcast by television stations in Canada be Canadian.
- Private stations (other than the CBC) are allowed to lower this to 50 percent between 6:00 p.m. and midnight.
- Canadian content requirements are also in force with regard to pay television and specialty channels.

What is Canadian content?

- The producer must be Canadian.
- The production itself must qualify for at least six out of 10 points. These points are earned based on the extent of the Canadian composition of the production team. Most members earn one point each (the two leading performers, the director of photography, the editor, the music composer) although the director and the screenwriter count for two points each. In addition, at least either the director or the screenwriter and one of the two leading performers must be Canadian.
- 75 percent of total remuneration paid to the production team must be paid to Canadians, not counting post-production expenses and money paid to the producer and director.
- Sports telecasts are considered Canadian if a Canadian producer is involved and provides a commentator, whether or not the match takes place in

Canada. In the event of a coverage of a match played abroad, the production will be considered Canadian content only when Canadian teams or Canadian athletes participate.

- When a broadcast is non-Canadian, and has been produced in one of Canada's official languages, and the audio portion has been converted into the other official language, it is considered Canadian content for up to 25 percent of its length.
- A non-Canadian production originally produced in a language that is not one of Canada's official languages and when the audio portion is supplied in one such language, it is considered Canadian content for up to one half of its length.
- Canadian drama productions aired between 7:00 p.m. and 10:00 p.m. (or at an appropriate viewing time in the case of children's programs) count for 1.5 times their actual length.[3]

These examples reflect the fact that any rule depends on definitions, which, like rules of origin in international trade agreements, in effect sometimes alter the practical meaning of the principles they are supposed to illustrate and uphold.

There is yet another sense in which success is ambiguous. Success means that Canadian-made offerings are indeed available. This is not to say, however, that such programs would necessarily continue to find an audience in Canada if the element of compulsion were removed and if viewers and listeners had expanded choice opportunities; nor, *a fortiori,* that they would necessarily find markets outside of the country. In other words, Canadian content is *aired* but is not necessarily *chosen.* An illustration of this is provided by comparing the distribution of viewing time between Canadian and foreign content for each linguistic viewing segment to the 60/40 content requirement discussed above. This is done in chart 8 which shows that, for anglophone audiences, the viewing coefficient for foreign content is more than four and a half times as high as that for Canadian content.

It would be misleading to believe that everything done in the field of film and television production is attributable to the national policy of protection and subsidization. For instance, in Quebec in 1992-1993, out of 31 feature films with a total budget of $116 million, 19 films benefited either from a tax credit or Telefilm support. The rest, almost 40 percent of films representing 55 percent of aggregate budgets, were produced with no government

chart 8

Viewing Coefficients by Origin of Content and Audience Segment

	CRTC Mandated Content Percentages (A)	Distribution Of Viewing Time (B)	Viewing Coefficients (B) ÷ (A) = C	Ratio Of Viewing Coefficients
Anglophone Segment				
Canadian Content:	60	25	0.4166	
				4.50
Foreign Content:	40	75	1.8750	
Francophone Segment				
Canadian Content	60	63	1.05	
				0.88
Foreign Content:	40	37	.92	

assistance of any kind. In Ontario, over the three-year period 1986-1989, 49 percent of all productions both for television and feature length films, that is to say 193 out of 390 productions, had no government help. On a Canada-wide basis for the period 1988 to 1992, 58 percent of the aggregate budgets of productions for television and 51 percent of feature film productions received no help from Telefilm Canada. This ratio reaches 60 percent when only English-language productions are considered. This establishes beyond any reasonable doubt that non-subsidized production of feature films and television programs is a viable activity in Canada. As we shall see later on, a substantial part of this non-subsidized production was targeted at the foreign, export market.

These results are all the more significant when one considers the great importance of public funding for the remainder of Canadian-produced films and television programs. Telefilm Canada's annual report for 1993 reveals that fully 67 percent of the total aggregated budgets of publicly supported feature films came from public funding, with foreign investors the second largest source at 13 percent. Financing from Canadian producers, distributors and broadcasters was next to insignificant on average, which means that the system of public support produces a situation where there is no incentive for producers and distributors to even think about getting a return on their investments.

For their part, the distributors can rely to a large extent on public funds for their own investments (upward of 70 percent). With producers and distributors both subsidized, and with broadcasters compelled by the CRTC policy to acquire Canadian content for broadcasting, the very existence of a non-subsidized and export-oriented sector is a remarkable demonstration of independent thinking, entrepreneurship and drive.[4]

The above reservations concerning the effectiveness of government support may sound churlish; however, in a context characterized by choice and where power is shifting from broadcasters to consumers, the limitations hinted at here regarding measurements of "success" may acquire immediate relevance. While most Canadians willingly support a national policy of encouraging Canadian content, the actual behaviour of the very same Canadians as individual consumers is inconsistent. In other words, as individual consumers of entertainment and information, Canadians will turn to what they think significant and interesting not because it is Canadian but because it corresponds to their needs and tastes. Consumers will not watch television programs just because those programs are Canadian-made; therefore, as their own individual choice acquires more and more relevance, the market will have an increasingly determinant impact on what gets produced.

Caution is Needed When Extrapolating From Past Success

Because Canadian cultural policy with regard to the electronic media and cinema is perceived to have been successful in the past, there is a strong temptation to respond to the challenge thrown up by the I-Way by extending to multimedia networks the legal obligations now applying to holders of broadcasting licences. Because public finances are in a position of acute stress to the point that even existing levels of expenditures may not be sustainable, "structural measures" (that is to say in rough terms, quotas enforced under the Broadcasting Act) are seen by some in Ottawa as the instrument of choice for the future.

In a strictly legal sense, there is no doubt that such an approach is feasible. An example of this point of view is provided by a recent CRTC decision (since placed under review by the Federal Cabinet) to declare exempt from CRTC oversight direct-to-home (DTH) television broadcasting by satellite when the satellite is majority-owned by Canadians and when more than half the channels carry Canadian content. This ruling dramatically extends to DTH a quota requirement that already applies to cable television licence holders with regard to their "first tier" of offerings. Such requirements are probably enforceable, since even a foreign-owned DTH beaming signals to Canadian dish antennas would need some sort of commercial presence in Canada for billing purposes and the sale or leasing of decoders. The real question is therefore not whether such policies are feasible – they are – but whether they can be effective.

The expansion of capacity for carriage up to and beyond the 500-channel universe, and the almost unfettered choice that will result from the transmission of compressed signals downloaded on demand to end-user terminal equipment, will make the notion of "shelf space" of no practical value with regard to the I-Way. If the range of choice on the I-Way becomes as wide as it is now for the print media in a well-stocked library, then whether or not a few shelves or even an entire section are devoted to Canadian content will have little or no impact on the use made of that content except in a few niche categories where there are no valid non-Canadian substitutes – such as Canadian newscasts and public affairs programs.

Unjustified Pessimism With Regard to Exports

One source of difficulty in any extension of present structural measures to the I-Way is based on the postulate that underlies these measures, namely that Canadian productions would not be freely preferred in competition with foreign productions, particularly in foreign markets. It is this postulate that must be seriously questioned. If valid, it would pose a fundamental challenge to the viability of public policy with respect to the maintenance of a distinct Canadian culture because it would be seriously at odds with the emerging technological environment. Again, it should be said that the policy could continue to be in force as a legal requirement long after its effectiveness had disappeared. At that point, the required production and distribution of Canadian content would be analogous to a tax on the Canadian I-Way and related activities – but a tax without countervailing benefits flowing to consumers in the sense that the cost involved in producing content that we do not use would have to be borne by Canadian I-Way end-users in the prices we would pay for the content we *did* use. It is questionable how long such a policy could be maintained.

However, if the postulate is correct, an even more serious consequence arises for the Canadian cultural industries themselves. There is a clear danger in generating content in Canada without taking into account a wider, partly non-Canadian, audience, because production and promotion budgets may be unnecessarily curtailed. This has too often been the case in the past, on the assumption that foreign markets were, almost by definition, closed or inaccessible for one reason or another to Canadian content producers. It is becoming clearer and clearer that this latter assumption can become a self-fulfilling prophecy; however, it is also an assumption that is contradicted by reality.

Canadian productions are exported to over 70 countries. In 1993, US buyers alone spent over US$100 million for the purchase of television programs produced in Canada. All major US channels, including ABC, CBS, Home Box Office, NBC, Nickelodeon, PBS, Show Time, the Disney Channel, the Family Channel, the Turner Network and the USA Network, are among Canada's clients. Indeed, the explosion in the demand for content spurred by the spread of cable television and, more recently, DTH appears to have created a situation where demand originating from the companies managing the distribution channels is rushing ahead of supply from established content producers, which are scrambling to fill all the capacity coming onto the market. This is an expanding opportunity that Canadian firms such as Atlantis Communications, Alliance Productions, Paragon Entertainment, Malo Films and Groupe Coscient are successfully exploiting. The expanding demand for content is also appearing in countries well beyond what could be considered Canada's traditional sphere (say, New Zealand, Australia, the United Kingdom and France) to include countries such as Germany, Sweden, Spain, Japan, Mexico and even China.[5]

Some of the above-mentioned production companies have been able to make inroads into US prime-time television. However, a few Canadian production companies seem to have particular success in exploiting a particular market niche, that of programming for children. Cinar Films has seen its production for children sold in 65 countries around the world. Nelvana, the largest producer of animation series in Canada, has an international reputation for high quality and has become the main supplier of animated films for the Saturday morning programming of three major US networks – ABC, CBS and Fox – and in the process has displaced Disney and Warner Brothers from first rank. Owl Communications and Productions Desclez are also active in this niche market.

Many Canadian film production companies are not just active in film production and co-production. Many have taken a more comprehensive look at the cultural industries sector and are marketing as a result their own and other producers' musical scores for films, rights to animated characters and interactive and CD-ROM games. Some are involved in video-cassette reproduction, post-production services, dubbing and subtitling and many round off their activities by managing distribution agreements for foreign producers in Canada. The names to remember in these peripheral markets are Cinar Films, Malo Films and Astral Communications.[6]

Upstream technical services have also provided a fertile feeding ground for several Canadian companies. In a short span of years, Softimage has emerged as a world leader in 3-D animation software. In 1993, the firm had 850 clients, of which 35 percent were American and 45 percent European. Among them were Sony, Nintendo, Walt Disney Studios, Steven Spielberg and George Lucas. Video games represent 35 percent of its present market. Discreet Logic is also active in 3-D animation software, having contributed to *The Coneheads, Super Mario Brothers, The Mask* and *Interview with the Vampire*. It is mostly active in the US market but has offices in London, Paris and Singapore, in addition to Los Angeles. Alias Research develops special effects software and is also active in the US.

There is another reason for considering audiences outside Canada when conceiving and producing Canadian cultural material. The expansion in consumer choice made increasingly possible by the I-Way will change the definition of the markets at which cultural content is aimed. This process is often referred to as the end of "broadcasting" and the rise of "narrowcasting," suggesting that the mass audience of the past will give way to segmented audiences, each amounting to a kind of affinity group, at least in terms of tastes and interests. This tendency is well illustrated in the magazine industry, which caters to every possible interest group from model railway hobbyists to bow hunting enthusiasts. Canada is already disadvantaged by a small population base divided between two main language groups with regard to the spreading of development and production costs over the total audience. In comparison with larger countries and especially the US, there is an order of magnitude of difference in audience size and a correspondingly greater difficulty in financing Canadian productions at a comparable level of quality and professionalism. The breaking up of mass markets into a host of small market segments only compounds the problem. It is clear from the point of view of commercial viability that unless these smaller market segments cut across national boundaries, most of them will be too small, within a single medium-size country, to support production costs at any level compatible with acceptable standards. On the other hand, "niche programmers will no longer need to produce enough content to fill a channel all day long, instead they can put any amount of it on a server and charge viewers as much as the market will bear."[7]

Such an industrial strategy will still allow producers to deal creatively with typically Canadian topics and issues. Canadian creators, performers and producers can be involved as fully, and certainly in a more viable way, in the implementation of such a strategy as they would be in the pursuit of a more narrowly focussed, Canada only, strategy.

Certainly, if we decide to base the vitality and development of Canadian cultural industries to a very significant extent on the need to be "chosen" by the viewing public, a new discipline will be imposed. It is quite clear that some business strategies would have to be reexamined and new roles connected with *distribution and promotion* significantly enhanced, as firms successful in the Canadian and international market have already well understood (we return to this point in greater detail in a later chapter). Moreover, given the terms of trade agreements entered into by Canada, the adoption of a strategy that depends to a significant extent on Canadians' success in penetrating foreign markets would mean that some traditional policy instruments would have to be reviewed. For instance, outright production subsidies might come to be considered as a handicap since they are bound to be criticized as an unfair advantage in at least some of those foreign markets. This is just one of the implications of shifting to a cultural industries policy that is outward looking and non-protectionist. More generally, there would be a need to ask ourselves the same question that Canadians in other sectors of economic activity have now grown accustomed to posing, namely, how competitive are we?

What About "Typically Canadian," Non-Exportable Content?

While proponents of a proactive cultural policy may concede that Canada's cultural industries could indeed prosper if they adopt an appropriate export-oriented strategy and can do so without government assistance, they may say that this only solves the job creation side of the issue, not the "cultural identity" side. In other words, is there a risk that content that is by its very nature only of interest to Canadians will become only a "niche market" – and a particularly unprofitable one because, by definition, a transnational audience for it does not exist?

Canadian news and public affairs programming is probably not at risk in this sense but "typically Canadian" dramatic series allegedly are, at least those in English. No one knows for sure.

Nothing, however, can subvert the fact that a substantial Canadian dramatic content production industry, making programs with obvious "typically Canadian" flavour, does exist and that it enjoys considerable audience support, even in other countries, and not only because of broadcasting policy. Many Canadian productions with Canadian themes have achieved considerable export sales: consider, for example, *Les filles de Caleb, Anne of Green Gables* and its sequel *Road to Avonlea, Due South, E.N.G.* and, more recently, *Million Dollar Babies.* Is "non-exportable, typically Canadian production" just an empty box? We suspect that it is – after all, if the American "Western" movie of cowboys and Indians has found a world audience and even prompted foreign pastiches, we have to admit that certain human types, be they American cowboys, Japanese samurai or a Canadian Mountie, may become universally recognizable types. Repeated exposure is part of the process whereby parochial or intensely local experiences become, so to speak, globally familiar icons: this is where access to distribution and clever promotion enter into the formula for successful diffusion.

Nor can anything subvert the right of any government to adopt a wilful approach on cultural issues and to refuse to give full sway to market forces if these were seen to be hostile. There is a genuine and wholly defensible justification for measures designed to maintain and enhance a distinct Canadian identity – an objective the authors of this paper heartily support. The questions raised here about the effectiveness of existing policies in an evolving context are not idle, gratuitous speculations but, on the contrary, are central to the continued pursuit of the same national objectives in the future.

If a decision was made that, on balance, led to continued government intervention, we suggest the resulting policy should be targeted at those segments and market niches where Canadian content is both an essential element of the national psyche and very unlikely to generate the threshold audience shares required in the emerging context of audience fragmentation.

Public resources that might be available for this purpose are unequal to the task of supporting production except in a few well-selected segments. For other, non-critical audience segments, and even with the best will in the world on the part of governments, there is no valid alternative to a Canadian content policy that relies upon a production strategy whereby the needs and tastes of non-Canadian viewers are fully taken into account. An idea we find attractive is to replace outright grants and Telefilm investments with a fiscal regime that would allow Canadian producers to reinvest their export profits in the production of targeted "non-exportable" content.

Canadian Competitiveness on The Global Information Highway

Few would quarrel with the assertion that the emergence of the global information highway creates a new challenge for Canadian competitiveness. However, there may be less unanimity as to what that expression means. How can we recognize whether Canada is competitive or not? Most importantly, how can competitiveness be achieved? To what extent is Canada's competitiveness merely an outcome of a myriad of individual decisions taken by particular firms or the outcome of correct policy decisions taken by government?

The simplest and probably best way to assess a country's competitiveness in a given sector is to measure its ability to be an exporter of the relevant goods and services – in this case, those related to the I-Way. There is a natural tendency to believe that, because of Canada's relatively small size, it is destined forever to be a net importer (or even worse a non-exporter) in the I-Way sector. However, this is simply not true, as we saw above.

There is in North America, Western Europe, East Asia and Australasia a total population of approximately one billion people who, to all intents and purposes and for the foreseeable future, constitute the only significant potential contributors to the global I-Way. By the end of the century, Canada's population of about 30 million people will represent a mere three percent of this total.

Unless we want to divorce ourselves from the rest of the developed world, an unthinkable hypothesis, it is to be expected that a very considerable portion of the total information content, entertainment, cultural products, application systems and services, software and equipment used for, or carried by, the I-Way will continue to come from outside Canada. Protectionism would be counterproductive and it is highly unlikely that Canadians would allow their governments to pursue such a course if only because it would severely damage other sectors' competitive positions as well as individual Canadians' quality of life.[8] However, an open market policy does not mean that Canada is condemned to be a net importer. If only Canada can obtain for itself more than a three percent share of this global highway-related services and products market, it can be a net exporter! The very size of that global market, far from being a threat, is an opportunity. This opportunity is the measure of the global information highway's potential to create wealth and jobs for Canada. A four percent global market share sounds like a very modest proposal but it probably means a very substantial increase in the present level of activity of companies in sectors associated with the I-Way. Anything above a nine percent share of the North American Free Trade Agreement (NAFTA) market carries the same implications.

No comprehensive evaluation seems to exist of the size of that global market or of Canada's success in penetrating it. Such an evaluation would be very useful, indeed vital. By enlisting the help of Statistics Canada, it might be possible to draw a comprehensive picture of information highway-related activities in this country, of Canada's balance of payments in these sectors and of the size and composition of the overall global market at least within and between those developed countries likely to have a significant presence.[9]

Many traditionally distinct sectors have to be brought in, at least in part, to draw this composite picture. We are dealing here with telecommunication services, broadcasting activities, a segment of electronic and telecommunications equipment manufacturers, compilers of data banks, applications software producers, multimedia services etc. What is Canada's competitive position in each of these segments? Is it possible to identify areas of strength, current or potential?

According to some estimates, already about 20 percent of information and educational content on US television channels is of Canadian origin! Canadian telecom equipment manufacturers have also occupied some significant niches. A better understanding of the statistics and an analysis of their implications would help give concrete meaning to a discussion of competitiveness.

For understandable reasons, our traditional concerns about competitiveness with regard to Canadian culture and content have been simultaneously too broad and too narrow. They have been too narrow in the sense that the national interest has sometimes been identified with the percentage of "made in Canada" entertainment programs that Canadians watched during peak-hour viewing times. There is more to Canadian culture and content than sitcoms. To assess Canada's competitiveness based on our ability to match offerings that come predominantly from the US and that enjoy a worldwide audience is to use an unfair standard. But it would be equally unfair and too broad to expect that Canada can be an effective competitor across the board for the whole range of services and products that contribute to the information highway.

The right balance lies somewhere between these two extremes. There is a large number of sub-sectors only a few of which can be expected to hold promise for Canadian initiative and entrepreneurship. In these, Canada should aim at cultivating a comparative advantage that will give it an overall surplus in its balance of payments for highway-related products and services, even as we bow to the realities of the international marketplace in most other sub-sectors. As we have seen, there already are indications of comparative success with regard to children's programs. The National Film Board's strong image in documentaries is another case in point. Canada's small-country, neutral-peacekeeper approach to controversial issues may give Canadian productions a competitive edge in global markets for information. Bowing to realities does not mean that Canadians should be absent entirely from other sub-sectors. For instance, made-in-Canada entertainment products have demonstrated capacity to win very substantial Canadian audiences and even limited foreign ones in exceptional cases.

This capacity must be recognized and, if possible, enhanced. All the same, it is not defeatist to recognize that, for instance, head-on competition with Hollywood is not necessarily the most promising path for Canadians to take.

The selection of promising sub-sectors where Canadian entrepreneurship can be rewarded not only in this country but in the global marketplace is primarily the business of individual firms, although data and analysis provided by government can certainly help firms make an educated guess. Beyond that, however, governments do make a difference, since by shaping support policies for Canadian creativity and entrepreneurship, government itself has to realize that its incentives, encouragement and support will be most effective if they can reinforce inherent strengths and emerging potentials rather than attempt to counteract overwhelming competition or create activity in areas where there is a lack of potential or commercial interest or both.

Competitiveness, therefore, depends on a synergistic deployment of private initiative, government leadership and incentives arising from a broadly similar vision and understanding of which sectors have the greatest potential for Canada. Much work ought to be done to develop such a common understanding.

However, competitiveness does not only presuppose making the right strategic choices in focussing resource deployment. In the global market for highway-related products and services, much depends on sustained promotional efforts in targeted markets and, above all, on effective access to those markets. International trade policies developed by the Government of Canada thus have a significant role to play in making sure that our trading partners' commitments under existing treaties (the General Agreement on Tariffs and Trade, the General Agreement on Trade in Services and the NAFTA) are ratified and enforced. In some cases, they need to be expanded and developed through further negotiations.

Broadcasting and telecommunications, the two pillars of the information highway, are everywhere regulated industries with a long tradition of at least *de facto* protectionism. The global market for cultural products, by its very nature, has a flip side which consists of the innate parochialism of culture even at the end of the 20th century. In this regard, the "global village" remains more a vision than a reality. Most large countries expect to be able to export their cultural products rather than import those of others. This is an effective barrier to Canadian offerings but it is a barrier that can be gradually overcome or eroded with determination and time.

What are the practical steps that might be recommended to foster Canadian competitiveness in the area of information highway-related products and services made in Canada?

- Enlist the help of Statistics Canada to draw a comprehensive and detailed picture of information highway-related activities, of the relevant world market and of Canadian performance or market shares in this market, segment by segment. Such data is an essential ingredient to an analysis of the industry's competitiveness.

- Using that data, establish a strategy to develop and promote Canadian content by identifying areas of present strength and assessing the future potential, sector by sector, through discussions with participants in each of the identified areas.

- Develop feasible stimulative measures, including public procurement programs, to enhance the potential, possibly by developing an application technology-oriented program that might parallel what CANARIE (a not-for-profit enterprise founded to promote greater competitiveness in Canada's information sector) is doing to help improve Canada's technological capabilities.

- Make sure that producers and distributors of Canadian content and applications have unlimited access to the international infrastructure of the global I-Way.

- Evaluate the need for continued support for "typically Canadian, non-exportable" offerings, target eventual support measures very specifically to defined market niches and segments and set up the support system in such a way that help in this regard is channelled toward those Canadian production firms that clearly demonstrate their command of marketing skills and abilities to penetrate markets.

- Develop training programs for cultural industry manpower to enhance awareness of I-Way opportunities, both technical and commercial, and to enhance, as required, the skills needed to exploit these opportunities.

Notes

1. In a 1989 directive, the European Union stipulated that a majority of television programs shown in Europe should be European-made. Some countries have not implemented the directive, known as "Television Without Frontiers," since its aim was to harmonize national legislation on this issue. An active campaign to regulate the use of the French language is being led by French National Assembly deputy Jacques Toubon, and a law was passed to this effect by the Assembly in August 1994. See Edmund Mortimer and David Buchan, "Watch your language," *The Financial Times,* November 29, 1994.

2. Statistics Canada, Cat. 87-208, 1987 to 1992. These figures come from the section entitled "Television Viewing."

3. CRTC, Public notice 1984-94 on "Recognition for Canadian Programs," August 15, 1984.

4. SECOR compilations from various trade sources and Telefilm Annual Report for 1993.

5. "Made for TV movies," *Report on Business Magazine,* May 1994.

6. Compiled by SECOR from trade sources, annual reports, direct contacts, prospectuses *etc.*

7. "Feeling for the future" in "A Survey of Television," *The Economist,* January 12, 1994.

8. An "open market" is an expression that only refers to the absence of economic barriers. It does not mean that certain I-Way content should not be barred (whether of Canadian or foreign origin) if they offend the country's sense of values, as was recently seen to be the case with regard to a particularly violent animated series aimed at children.

9. Statistics Canada has initiated a revision of its 1980 Standard Industrial Classification. To be completed for 1997, the revision constitutes an attempt for the first time to create comparable economic data for all NAFTA countries. This creates an opportunity for the broadcasting, telecommunications, computer services and information technology sectors to gain a better picture of their relative position.

FIVE

INFORMATION HIGHWAY
MARKET INTERMEDIARIES

Both broadcasting and telecommunications are entering an era where, when seen from the end-user's point of view, there is vastly greater choice but where that choice brings with it its own difficulties. The end-user needs help choosing wisely and efficiently among what will end up being an almost infinite variety of offerings. With a myriad of possibilities, the end-user needs at the very least a map but more probably a guiding hand. Information overload can be intensely frustrating, as anyone who has lost a misfiled piece of paper can testify. Hence the major benefit expected from the I-Way, very extensive choice, is not without problems, and these need to be effectively addressed and managed.

However, the problem of choice does not only arise for the end-user; it also becomes a problem for the generator of content, since access to the highway is meaningless unless the existence of a particular content, its qualities and relative attractiveness are somehow advertised. Undoubtedly, data retrieval systems and various types of access software can help the end-user but it would be naive to believe that this is only a technical problem that will be totally wiped away by a technical solution. Putting together end-user requirements and content producers' offerings is not just a technical problem but also a business problem. Choice of content means that there will be a market for contents. This market, in turn, will create room for market intermediaries.

Exploding choice of content is creating for broadcasting what open, unbundled competition is about to create for the carriage of telecommunications. In fact, competition has already created an intermediary business to help large end-users of telecommunications services to wisely and efficiently purchase what they need from a variety of competing providers using a variety of technologies. With the scope for competition expanding all the time, these choices will become more and more complex. Choice is about more than just price: end-users are concerned about various technical characteristics, discount patterns or enhanced quality. All this needs to be assessed and compared in relation to an increasing number of suppliers. Recently, the emergence in Canada of full-fledged and easy-to-use competition for long-distance voice services has created an interesting and constantly shifting problem for individual residential customers. The choices offered to large business users are even more complex, by several orders of magnitude. The market for telecommunications has become so sophisticated that intermediaries are called for.

In this chapter and in chapters 6 and 7, we attempt to give a comprehensive account of what this new intermediary role is for both content and telecommunications. We also try to indicate how much of a change the emerging system represents and to describe the extent of the change in behaviour that it entails. We also address the question of what may be lost in the process, and conclude by drawing some regulatory implications.

If the words "intermediation" or "intermediaries" sound too forbidding and abstract, the reader might like to think of *brokers*. However, this term suggests merely a trading (buying and reselling) role, whereas the true intermediary in addition selects, brands, packages and customizes the product (whether it be content or transmission capacity), thereby adding value.

The Role of Market Intermediaries for Content

Let us go back to the publishing industry analogy. Every year, tens of thousands of new titles are published by hundreds of publishers in North America. As we have seen, this is a similar situation to the one that could eventually prevail on the I-Way for content of all kinds in a common digital format.

How do certain books get bought and read? The answer is that books have to be promoted. Contrary to the situation of television before the spread of cable, where it used to be sufficient for a program to be selected for prime-time exposure to be watched by millions of viewers, publishers must actively promote the books they produce. For this purpose, a variety of means is used, including paid advertising, autograph sessions by the authors, book reviews in newspapers of note *etc.*

An interesting question – although perhaps unduly focussed on the interests of present-day broadcasters – is whether or not in a world of unrestricted choice "general-interest channels" will survive.[1] It would be easy to assume that specialty channels and "narrowcasting" to narrowly defined audience segments would spell the end of the general-interest channels. There is considerable plausibility to this notion in a world of 500 channels, or even an infinite number of channels: a general-interest channel targeted at a broadly defined audience is bound to be seen as the second-best option for almost all viewers. The culmination of the channel-zapping behaviour of a large part of the television audience in the age of cable television would find its ultimate expression on the I-Way. The multiplicity of individual choices allowed cannot possibly be matched by any offering designed with everyone in view – young and old, literate and semi-literate *etc*. However, it might be premature to proclaim the disappearance of the "passive viewer." Consider that the universe of almost infinite choice that is promised will require a correspondingly proactive viewer. With so many offerings to choose from, zapping is no longer a practical option and many viewers may be happy to delegate their power to choose – although it is unclear to whom and to what extent they would be prepared to so delegate. In other words, the I-Way's cornucopia of choice will certainly call for a redefinition of the general-interest channel; yet it may not quite spell its demise.

This is particularly true if general-interest channel programmers (and indeed all other programmers of I-Way offerings) managed to overcome the reduced salience of scheduling as a tool for programming. Choosing the time at which to view a particular offering is perhaps the most fundamental dimension of consumer choice, and one the video recorder has not been able to successfully provide for all consumers, the overwhelming majority of whom have yet to find a programming technology they can easily master. Both general-interest and specialty-interest channels, the latter perhaps more than the former, will thus need to cope with a new dimension of content distribution activity – namely, the desire and indeed requirement of consumers to be able to view any material at a time of their own choosing.

This has important implications for the activities of promotion and distribution of content over the I-Way. As soon as producers and distributors of content lose their mastery over timing, the notion of prime time, as well as the notion of shelf space in that prime time, become empty boxes. The value, in economic terms, of any content can no longer be derived from the prescribed timing of the presentation but solely from its inherent qualities. Prime time, being scarce, was a very precious commodity and it commanded premium prices. This is perhaps the most important way in which the I-Way alters both power relationships and the precise location along the value creation chain where most value is added. In the old – and still surviving – model, ownership of the infrastructure determines "ownership" of the end-user clientele. With tomorrow's I-Way, the "ownership" of the clientele will go to the selector, packager, promoter and brander of the content, in short, to the value-adding intermediary.

The consequence of all this is to point suppliers in the direction of improved marketing techniques, including branding. With prime time no longer an indicator or a source of value, the consumer in her search for what she needs or enjoys most will probably be guided by the brand image of a distribution enterprise, associated in her own mind with a well-defined domain of interest, a certain style or a certain pitch. There are still science fiction-like references in the literature to the eventual emergence of intelligent, custom-made programming and program selection services designed to perfectly match a single individual's preference pattern. This will no doubt be attempted in time. But just as likely, and certainly much more probable in the near to medium term given issues of cost efficiency, is the development of brand names linked to perceived performance attributes; these will just as strongly help to *shape* the tastes of substantial segments of the viewing public as they themselves initially *reflect* inherent differences in taste. Walt Disney Studios, in sharp distinction to other Hollywood film production companies, has successfully created such a brand image by offering films for a "family audience" with no violence, positive morality and muted sexuality. What is important to the branding function of an I-Way intermediary is not that Walt Disney itself produces theses films but that it selects and markets them. On behalf of individual investors, the mutual fund industry has simplified portfolio selection and management strategies, not only on the basis of comparative performance but also of a prior choice between major categories of investments such as bonds *versus* equities, domestic securities *versus* foreign, ethical funds, growth funds *etc.* Mind-boggling choice among millions of possible investments is thereby reduced to a relatively simpler choice among a limited number of packages.

With choice possible among innumerable possibilities, the I-Way in the first instance creates a challenge for the individual consumer. However, that challenge will from the start be met in part by the activities of proactive intermediaries, diligently pursuing market segmentation, customer profiling and segment-based content sifting. Not only will such offerings find a more willing market among end-users but these customer profiles can then provide an attractive base for targeted publicity and promotional efforts to well-defined audience segments, thereby generating publicity and other revenue. This is very different from the publicity revenue that general-interest channels have been able to tap in the past but are finding increasingly difficult to exploit. The point of all this is that the I-Way creates a new market. Beyond content, it is a market for choice of content, a value that will increasingly have to be added to the content itself. The I-Way content intermediary will, in a manner of speaking, play the hightech equivalent of the friendly video store owner.

Such intermediaries do not entirely belong to the future. Existing data retrieval firms have seen their business prospects appraised upward in the past year or so and their potential role in providing a road map and even a pilot to navigate the I-Way has begun to become apparent. These firms provide access to a multiplicity of data bases and, in particular but only up to a point, to Internet. These include CompuServe (with two to three million clients), America Online (one million), Prodigy (two million) and several others. However, these existing firms behave more as intermediaries for *access* to data banks than as intermediaries for *content*. Reuters, the financial data company, is a better example of a content provider; so is Dialog, a business information services group. The intermediation function has several overlapping layers; among these, the layers that are closest to end-user requirements are associated with a bigger contribution to value added than those closest to the infra-structure. An example of the latter are resellers of infrastructure capacity, which only perform an "arbitrage function" by buying wholesale capacity at low prices and reselling it retail for a somewhat higher price.

The I-Way comes into its own when it provides interactive services; this is where the resources of contents and applications producers and the potential of telecommunications are joined to greatest effect. This is also where inter-mediaries can find the best context to provide added value and where they can maximize their contributions relative to those of either content providers or infrastructure operators.

Would such intermediaries inherently have gatekeeper power? They will have to spend resources on acquisition and selection of material, branding, development of procedures and software to facilitate access and promotion. All these are demanding tasks requiring a large dose of innovation given rapidly evolving markets; therefore, for all that, this is a business associated with substantial risks. To offset the risks, intermediaries must be in a position to acquire, lease or in some other way contract for copyrightable material and thereby preclude potential users from having access without paying; otherwise, it is difficult to see why they would accept the risks associated with large investments in the promotional expenses needed to "create a market" for the material. The sometimes conflicting requirements of universal access, common carriage, competition and ownership rights that will ensure an optimum development of the intermediary function are something that needs careful consideration, and we return to this point in a later section. The issue of competition among intermediaries, the lowering of barriers to entry, the issue of copyright management as well as the question of ownership and inter-operability of end-user terminal equipment are all key in this context.

Market Intermediaries for Transfer Services

In the field of telecommunications, where, initially, no or very few facilities-based competitors were present, resellers have played a very significant role in squeezing distribution margins. However, with wholesale margins deliberately inflated through the absence of rate rebalancing and as a result still quite high for long-distance traffic, the competitive frontier is gradually moving over to that area. With the pressures growing in most western countries to unbundle network facilities, these margins are next in line for the onslaught of competition. In any case, with some resellers acquiring for themselves facilities that they own outright, competitive options for telecommunications are growing more numerous, even within a given technology, while additional alternative technologies are regularly coming on stream.

Therefore, for telecommunications as well as broadcasting, choices are widening and multiplying to such a degree that large end-users feel more and more the need for sophisticated purchasing officers or for the advice of telecommunications consultants. In comparison shopping, more than price is involved: quality, reliability and a constantly expanding number of enhanced services facilities are also factors. These choices, until now the domain of large business purchasers, will soon confront individual customers. In the case of video signals, consumers will be asked to choose among traditional cable television, direct-to-home satellite services, telephone companies' video dial tones and possibly other options. With regard to residential telephone services, emerging options are fixed line and cellular as well as Personal Communications Systems (the third generation of cellular telephony); at the same time, customers will need to choose among several carriers offering various packages for local, long-distance and overseas services. Again, this points to the need for intermediaries.

Traditional carriers of telecommunications can attempt to provide integrated services themselves. However, they are bound to offer second-best options to the extent that they fall prey to a very natural tendency to prolong the economic life of their own sunk assets, even when new emerging technologies might be preferable on the basis of the consumer's own best interest. As a result, market share attrition for the incumbents is almost inevitable and will accelerate when more and more lines of business become competitive with remaining "monopoly" services. These traditional players will see a decline both in their relative importance and in their ability to cross subsidize. The recent CRTC decision (94-19) mandating unbundled tariffs for telecommunications transmission services and switching facilities has committed Canada to allowing the full play of competitive forces, segment by segment. This policy direction was further reinforced by a Cabinet Order-in-Council mandating the CRTC to hold public hearings on the I-Way. The order contained a clear policy direction, including a decision that cable and telecom facilities and capacity should "be made available for lease, resale and sharing by service providers and other carriers on a non-discriminatory basis."[2] These policies, in effect, open the door to independent intermediaries.

The distinction between competitive and monopoly services is one that has driven much of the policy debate in Canada and in other countries. Without wanting to downplay the importance of the distinction in a period of transition from monopoly to generalized full competition, it is nonetheless true that the realities of the emerging world of telecommunications impose another type of distinction against which the issue of "competition" versus "monopoly" pales in significance.

That other distinction – between *service provision* and *infrastructure operations* – already exists today, at least conceptually. In telecommunications but also in most transport industries, very expensive and "lumpy" infrastructure is used. In some sectors, a tradition has built up of mixing the two businesses together; in other sectors, by contrast, the two businesses are clearly distinguished. For instance, in road haulage, infrastructure (i.e., roads) is provided by the state, while businesses of all types – local and long-distance goods transporters, local and inter-city bus services as well as drivers of private cars – contribute to the fixed costs through assessed charges (licence fees related to size of vehicle and purpose of the business) and usage-related fees (gasoline taxes and tolls). It never entered anyone's mind to require a trucking company to build its own road, probably because roads existed before trucking businesses emerged. This, however, is not a universal principle: consider, for example, that logging firms build their own access roads to reach the resource and, apart from campers, fishermen and hunters, they will be the sole users. In general, however, many competing businesses share the same transportation infrastructure. This is also true, of course, in the airline indus-try. The same airports, navigational aids, air control and weather services are used by competing airlines. In some very busy airports, some air terminals may be built by a single airline or a group of several. In general, however, the principle of common use of facilities applies whether or not the facilities in question are provided by a public or commercial corporation. The same principles apply to commercial shipping.

In all these sectors, any other *modus operandi* would only increase costs and penalize the consumer. It would also create enormous surplus capacity, a problem that would be more acutely experienced in Canada, with its huge territory and comparatively small population.

With regard to railways, the situation, as we all know, is different. Traditionally, each railway company has built its own railways and therefore found itself in the dual business of operating an infrastructure and providing a service. There are exceptions to this rule. In Canada, ViaRail is now an inde-pendent provider of passenger rail transport services, using the infrastructure of one or the other of the cargo railway companies' tracks for a fee. The same system prevails in the US. In Europe, the *Compagnie Internationale des wagons-lits* has long been operating luxury train services between major cities in different countries using state railway infrastructure. There could be substantial competi-tion for rail transport in Canada if there were a distinction made between infrastructure and services (as is the case for air or road transport). It is indeed surprising that this option does not seem to have been considered, even in the context of the proposed merger of Canadian National and Canadian Pacific operations in Eastern Canada – a proposal rejected by the federal government.

The existing arrangement for railways appears distinctly sub-optimal. In exchange for the dubious advantage of operating a duopoly (but in reality a monopoly of rail services in many regions), CN and CP have had to shoulder the full cost of an infrastructure in competition with subsidized road trans-port. When railway companies failed to be competitive, subsidies were paid to make up for losses; however, this provided a poor incentive to increase productivity. Opening up railway *services* to competition, with common infra-structure subsidized if need be to the same extent as roads are, would have made better sense. Certainly the UK government seems to think so: this is the system it is putting in place in the process of privatizing British Rail.

Telephone companies are, in this regard, very much like railway companies. That this is the case can, perhaps, be traced back to the time when rail and telecommunications were regulated by the same agencies. It has always been taken for granted that telephone services had to be provided by companies supplying the infrastructure. However, building and maintaining an infrastructure are something very different from providing telephone services to individuals and businesses. With an expanded array of services beyond the plain own telephone services of old and, in particular, with more and more software-based services leading to greater scope for competition between telephone companies and resellers, there is obvious merit in the notion of cutting the tie that binds infrastructure to service provision. Some of the competing offerings in the telecommunications sector no longer even need to use the traditional infrastructure.

In a period when the quality of services to consumers and responsiveness to their needs become paramount there is much to be said for a form of organization in the telecommunications industry that would allow a large number of medium-size competitors to provide the relevant services.

The room for innovation on the telecommunications side of the I-Way is just as important as it is on the content or, to use present terminology, the "broadcasting" side. There are hundreds of new applications that will be developed to exploit the potential of wide-band, low-cost telecommunications. Things thus can be speeded up enormously: the creative energy of many innovators and entrepreneurs could be liberated by removing the shackles of having to build or acquire infrastructure facilities. This is a serious barrier to entry in the market and an unnecessary one. Of course, entrepreneurs should not be barred from owning a piece of infrastructure when that strategy appears justified. However, it should not be a requirement and the option should be one that can be exercised selectively – i.e., in order to buy just that one piece of equipment that can make a difference to services delivery.

The provision of infrastructure is something that can be resolved for the telecommunications industry roughly in the way it has been resolved for the road transport or air transport industries – namely, by separating infrastructure from services. Infrastructure development requires huge capital investments: investment is lumpy and, with low population density, there is not room for too many competitors.

Some US telephone companies have already understood this and are attempting to respond. Rochester Telephone Company, now called Frontier Corporation, has put forward a plan that will split its activities between two separate corporations, called respectively R-Net (the infrastructure company) and R-Com (the service company).[3] The infrastructure company will provide services to the service company on a non-discriminatory basis but would also provide infrastructure to all R-Com competitors. This plan received regulatory approval on October 13, 1993, and will go into effect on January 1, 1995.

Already announced competitors for local service include Time-Warner and the MFS Communications Company.[4] In the US context, Rochester Telephone was keen to establish a competitive structure for the provision of local telephone services and thus earn the right to provide long-distance services to its customers. Whatever the precise motivation (and the case would vary country by country), the credibility of the proposal rests on the feasibility of the distinction between infrastructure and service, something the company believes is beyond question. The same assumption lies behind a similar though distinct effort by Ameritech, the regional Bell operating company for the US Mid-West, to split itself into two parts. This proposal goes even further than that of Rochester Telephone.[5] For instance, Ameritech proposes to lease individual segments of its carriage network, such as local loops or trunks as well as rights of way. It is even proposing to unbundle its Signalling System 7 (SS7) call set-up capabilities, thereby permitting competitors access to its signalling network without having to subscribe to the company's transport or switching services.

This last feature borrows a concept from a PhD dissertation by Stephen J. Downs, who asserts that network architecture that can be used by ATM technology opens up an entirely new opportunity for an optimal structuring of the telecom industry, an opportunity that public policy should eagerly seize upon.[6] By conceiving SS7 networks as a distinct component that can be unbundled, Ameritech has taken the first step toward separating the signalling network from the transfer network, a move that may lead to the gradual implementation of the network control principles known as the "intelligent network." Through ATM networks, control logic is separated from local switches, thereby opening up opportunities for expanded choice in use of network control services, a precondition for multimedia, multiparty telecommunications. The greater sophistication of the signalling function in the I-Way reflects the much greater complexity of signalling requirements associated with a multitude of modes from voice telephony to data transmission, video signals *etc.* To quote Downs:

> By the time the public telephone network has evolved into a public broadband network, it will no longer be recognizable as a telephone network – it will be something entirely new.
>
> (...)
>
> The adoption of ATM technology into public networks will make possible a shift in the traditional roles of network providers from delivering vertically integrated specialized services, such as telephony or cable

television channels, to providing more fundamental communications building blocks. These building blocks can be used by end users or independent service providers to create new services or to support emerging communications applications. The unbundling of the traditional network functions into these basic building blocks offers a new role for traditional carriers – the role of network wholesaler, supplying basic, service-independent communications capacity to service providers, applications developers and systems integrators.[7]

Summary

The I-Way creates, and is itself the result of, expanding opportunities. It makes immediately available at extremely low cost an almost infinite variety of content from all over the world; in short, it erases the economic significance of distance. Computer applications themselves form part of the expanding communications sector and add value by making all this content accessible where and when it is wanted and by providing even more options with regard to efficient transfer. In all these cases, the requirement to choose creates a new environment and a new challenge. This challenge, in turn, gives rise to new functions, new ways to make the choices and to match resources to preferences and needs. Organizations of one type or another have always mediated between content creators and complex technical infrastructure on the one hand and the end-users on the other. In the old paradigm, these tasks were relatively simple; this is no longer so. Control over some pieces of infrastructure once gave some of the players enormous powers to preempt end-users' choices. This era is coming to an end, as technical innovation and competition erode these power centres. As a result, intermediary functions will no longer play an auxiliary role but will occupy centre stage. Could intermediaries for telecommunications and intermediaries for content converge? How will each or both operate? These are the questions we consider next.

Notes

1. Presentation by the Canadian Association of Broadcasters to the Working Group on Canadian Content and Culture of the Advisory Council on the Information Highway, November 17, 1994.

2. Order-in-Council, PC 1994-1689, October 8, 1994 announced on October 11, 1994 by Ministers Michel Dupuy and John Manley.

3. State of New York Public Service Commission "Petition of Rochester Telephone Corporation for Approval of Proposed Restructuring Plan, Case 93-C-0103 Joint stipulation and agreement," 57 pages plus appendices. See also in the same docket "Direct testimony" of Nina W. Cornell on behalf of MCI Telecommunications Corporation, July 11, 1994.

4. *Telecommunications Reports,* Vol. 60, no. 42 (October 17, 1994), p. 1. and Vol. 60, no. 43 (October 24, 1994), p. 17.

5. David J. Teece, "The Inter LATA Restriction in light of changing technology, increased competition, strengthened regulation and Ameritech's Customer First Plan," a supporting document to Ameritech's motions to remove the decree's inter-exchange restriction submitted to the US Department of Justice, US District Court, DC, Case No 82-0192.

6. Stephen J. Downs, "Asynchronous Transfer Mode and the Public Broadband Networks – the Policy Opportunities," *Telecommunications Policy,* Vol. 18, no. 2 (March 1994), pp. 114-36.

7. Downs, "Asynchronous Transfer Mode," pp. 120-21.

THE SERVICE VERSUS
INFRASTRUCTURE DISTINCTION:
HOW WOULD IT WORK?

In preceding chapters, we argued that Canada ought to encourage the emergence and development of a non-vertically integrated industrial structure for I-Way core participants. We also argued that, in an environment characterized by immediacy, consumer-driven choice and inevitable market segmentation, there was a growing need for a highly entrepreneurial, competitive domestic industry, particularly with regard to content generation and distribution. We further underlined that distribution was a key activity but one that should no longer be driven by the technological support infrastructure but rather by commercial considerations. Distribution should be seen as a systematic and proactive effort to earn the privilege of being chosen by consumers, both in Canada and abroad.

All of these concerns can be met by the emergence of a strong intermediary role for both content and telecommunications services, as was explained in the preceding chapter. In those pages, we emphasized the *concept* of an intermediary. This is insufficient to make plain the various implications that the *implementation* of this concept would entail. As we will now see, there are consequences both in terms of industry structure and commercial behaviour; in particular, questions arise with regard to the economic impact of the services *versus* infrastructure distinction.

Structural Considerations

Any system provides intermediaries between raw inputs and the final consumer. Readers may then wonder what is new in our call for intermediary functions. They might point to existing organizations that already play such a role. For instance, cable television companies can claim they mediate between broadcasters in the strict sense (i.e., television networks) and the consumer. Indeed, their role has gradually expanded to include distribution of independently produced specialty channels, community programming and even non-programming services.

However, this distribution role is a far cry from the competitive market intermediary function described above. Cable television companies distribute signals in the same sense that the electricity grid distributes electricity – from a position of monopoly, from a position of power *vis-à-vis* consumers. Their clients do not choose them but are "given" to them because they are the owners of the only technical infrastructure (namely the coaxial connection) presently capable of carrying video signals to the home. As a result of this position of power, they do have a penetration strategy, (i.e., they try to sign up as close as possible to 100 percent of the homes passed by their cables), but they have little use for marketing strategies, market segmentation, product selection, competitive pricing, branding or any of the means by which competitive, market-driven enterprises manage to acquire or maintain market share.

In the emerging competition among transmission channels, whether coaxial cable, DBS/DTH satellites, video dial tone or even cellular vision, the approach of cable television companies is not to try to select the channel that would minimize cost to their subscribers or provide extra options or optimize value for money, but to adopt a defensive stance *vis-à-vis* the sunk capital represented by their cable networks. The link of cable television companies to a given infrastructure, so important to their financial performance, largely inhibits them from graduating from their traditional role as distributor tied to a given infrastructure to the role of market intermediary.

Once freed of the link to that infrastructure, video distribution companies (they could hardly then call themselves cable television companies) would have an open mind *vis-à-vis* various transmission channels; however, because they now would be in a competitive environment, they would have to acquire similarly competitive instincts and behaviour *vis-à-vis* content itself.

The present confusion of roles for cable television companies also exists for broadcasters and telephone companies. Broadcasters not only generate content or programming but they own and operate off-air broadcasting facilities. Indeed, they owe their status as producers of programs to their ownership of the facilities used to fill their assigned segment of the scarce frequency spectrum. Here again, infrastructure dominates program generation. Infrastructure is the barrier, the obstacle, the prerequisite – not only in terms of the time, expenses and risk of obtaining and renewing a licence but in terms of the sheer amount of capital resources needed to acquire or build the facilities in the first place. Similarly, telephone companies, for a long time considered "natural monopolies," were defined first and foremost by the telephone poles, the rights-of-way, the switching centres, the microwave towers that, taken together, entitled them to provide services to consumers.

The dominance of hardware in both telecommunications and broadcasting is a striking characteristic of these sectors. But it is this very characteristic that is challenged by the I-Way. By multiplying technological options, thereby creating a technological environment appropriate to foster competition, the paradoxical result of technological change is to overturn the previous dominance of technology as a rationale for business organization and structure in the two sectors. There is now no valid reason why there could not be many telephone companies in the same city even for local services, many competing businesses in the market for packaging, selecting and marketing video content or any other kind of content. The insistence that no one can be in these businesses unless they can afford hundreds of millions of dollars or even billions of dollars in upfront capital investment to build parallel facilities to those that presently exist has become anachronistic and counter-productive.

Technology makes possible the separation of service provision from infrastructure operation. But what technology makes possible, government policy should turn into a requirement.

The job of devising content, programs, applications or whatever else this infrastructure can carry requires innovation, creativity and ease of entry and exit so that virtually everyone with talent can have a kick at the can without undue risk – except, of course, the risk of being disappointed. This open access to the I-Way for potential content providers would work to the greater benefit of society as a whole. Public policy would seek to make the world safe for small and medium-size enterprises: after all, the presence of integrated giants relying on the cash flow from their concurrent ownership of huge capital-intensive facilities may have a deterrent effect on entry into the industry by smaller competitors. It may bias outcomes or would at best be a source of endless regulatory ambiguity and conflicts.

If Canadians are to have a maximum opportunity to contribute as creators, producers and distributors of content, the best solution we can imagine is an environment made congenial for small- and medium-size business enterprises. Maintaining the Canadian ownership of such firms is easier if they are not required – indeed if they were prohibited from – owning capital-intensive facilities.

If that is accepted, and in light of the current fiscal climate, one could question whether public expenditure directed, for instance, at the CBC would not be better targeted using our frame of reference. To be more specific, the CBC is not only a producer of content but also an owner and operator of broadcast facilities across the country. Is it not time to separate those two functions? The production side of CBC is in effect a "real-time" analog to the National Film Board. With the multiplication of video-transmission channels, would it not be better for the CBC to contract out the role of facilities operator? What with cable television, telephone companies, video dial-tone and satellites, is there a future for off-air broadcasting? It uses up a lot of scarce frequency spectrum that might be put to better uses. But more importantly, the public resources used for this infrastructure function, which are making no specifically Canadian contribution as far as one can see, could be channelled to the production side or, at least, help limit the damage arising from shrinking budgets.

Private broadcasters are similarly situated astride two businesses. With the advent of digital radio and the ensuing effective multiplication of radio channels, radio broadcasters will acquire a totally different set of opportunities, some far removed from cultural content of any kind. Among our radio broadcasters, how many have the background, the dynamism and the capital to fully exploit this new capacity?

The relevance of the argument to separate content distribution from infrastructure may not be apparent now, in a context where all firms operating facilities of any kind in the broadcasting and telecommunications fields are overwhelmingly Canadian-owned. However, as these sectors move from a relatively sheltered era of monopoly or quasi-monopoly to a competitive situation, the financial viability of all existing players is far from assured. Assume just a few bankruptcies among them and ask yourself how many Canadian purchasers, other than the present players, would step forward in any open post-bankruptcy auction?

The alternative approach to ours would see full facilities-based competition among integrated I-Way firms, encompassing every step from content generation through distribution to infrastructure ownership. This implies, as a necessary corollary, huge capital requirements for start-up and development. Such huge investments would be made in a sector that is already undergoing rapid transformation as a result of the combined thrust of technological change, a changing market structure and unforeseeable new sources of competition. All this translates into high risks for investors. For the new entrants, the combination of huge capital requirements and high risks is one that the Canadian capital market may not find entirely to its liking.

To sum up, the I-Way is shifting the leverage point for both broadcasting and telecommunications away from infrastructure and toward competitive commercial distribution. The firms that can best match both human and material resources to end-user requirements will be those market intermediary firms whose ability to respond to change is not bound to the deadweight of undepreciated capital assets. That is the major shift that is required in business strategies and government policy to make the I-Way successful – not just financially but in terms of realizing the true potential of making a difference in our lives; to fulfil, without dilution, the implicit promise of the highway in terms of immediacy and customer choice.

Behavioural Implications

There is a dramatic behavioural shift implied in moving from a model of content distribution that is leveraged by a power relationship based on ownership of quasi-monopolistic facilities to a market intermediary model where the challenge to competing intermediaries is to have their offerings selected by consumers. An I-Way market intermediary is a commercial business. An example of what this means can be found in the current practices of the US cinema industry. For many of the so-called box office "blockbusters" such as *Jurassic Park,* promotion of content becomes almost an adjunct to huge sales promotion efforts involving T-shirts, plastic dinosaurs, licence contracts for use of the name *etc.,* the dollar value of which far exceeds total box office receipts. To be successful, these strategies require saturation coverage of the domestic market, aimed at creating a marketing aura that fuels demand for derivative products even among people who have not yet seen the film and who might never do so. Such heights of entrepreneurial activism are certainly not possible in all market segments; perhaps not in any outside the mass teenage market. However, the almost caricatural features of the *Jurassic Park* example help make a point about the sort of entrepreneurial culture that is required for success in a world of choice and global markets.

This call for a behavioural revolution within the Canadian cultural industries will probably be seen as something close to an obscenity by many people. Before we summarily dismiss this "excessive commercialism," we also have to be careful to note that films such as *Terminator 2* and *Jurassic Park* were cultural products with a world audience that showcased the skills of a small Canadian software company, Softimage. If creativity and inventiveness are what we are truly after and if a world market is necessary for us to realize the potential that Canadian individuals and business possess, then these commercial ventures should not be despised. Creative talent may want to maintain its purity, but it could only do so at a cost – one this country may not be able to afford. Like all living things, unless creative people are prepared to adapt to their environment (since they have little hope of fundamentally changing that environment, which in every way – demographic, technological and economic – transcends them), they are doomed.

The commercial dimension of cultural products is something that we can only ignore at our peril. First of all, within Canada itself, "commercial success" is just another expression to designate end-user choice. Without end-user choice, shelf-space (and hence quota) requirements are a delusion. End-user choice is not just a measure of success at the distribution phase, it is also a reasonable expectation, a *sine qua non* of production itself, since otherwise financing, at least from private sources, would not be available. Of course, content production may be subsidized or "sponsored"; however, the political viability of subsidies, at least in the medium to long-term, is similarly dependent on a measure of end-user choice.

All of the above is not a counsel for despair in relation to the existing Canadian policy of support to the arts and in particular to film and television industries. There is some truth in the assertion that supply creates its own demand. For cultural products there is a special feedback mechanism whereby, through repeated exposure, a public learns, so to speak, what to expect and develops an acquired taste for certain content and presentation. This is not limited to publicly supported content generation, since even commercial strategies are predicated on these same mechanisms. Each country's film industry cultivates a certain style to which its audience becomes accustomed, and educated into wanting more.

The role of public funding of film and television production is clear: to make sure that this feedback mechanism between supply and demand for Canadian content is properly fed and never interrupted. Canadian content for this purpose acquires a specific meaning: it does not refer to all content made in Canada using Canadian creators and Canadian talent because such productions targeted at global market segments can be expected to have a good chance of being successful without public support. The focus of public funding should be content that is Canadian by reason of its subject matter – by definition only appealing to a Canadian audience. This audience, of course, is smaller than that for programs winning not only domestic but international favour as well. In other words, public funding is justified only where it compensates not weakness on the supply side but weakness on the demand side. That weakness cannot be a form of "there are not enough viewers" but only "there are not enough Canadian viewers for this typically Canadian offering."

Our point here has been that the I-Way requires a new type of behaviour. More commercial instincts, more aggressive pursuit of market share and more ingenuity in pursuing ways of making money can help carry the huge costs and efforts required in promoting content in a competitive marketplace. Having I-Way market intermediaries in an arm's length position *vis-à-vis* infrastructure operations is only the first requirement for such a change. The other requirement is a change in behaviour and an underlying change in business culture.

Competition between Infrastructure Operators

The segregation between the intermediaries that provide services on the I-Way and, on the other hand, operators of the facilities that together make up the I-Way is designed to lower entry barriers into the I-Way intermediary sector, both with regard to content and, of course, facilities too. It is important to understand the sort of market for facilities that would exist under this system. As we propose to demonstrate, not only is the segregation beneficial for the intermediation business but it also holds out the promise of creating a competitive environment where, from society's perspective, one can more easily attain an optimal deployment and use of expensive, capital-intensive infrastructure.

Even without the segregation of services provision from infrastructure operations, there exists an increasing measure of competition among facilities. The competition is to some extent lopsided in the sense that it results from the present need of service providers to use their own facilities if they are not to be overwhelmed by vertically integrated competitors. This creates a paradox. Competition in services is driven by infrastructure, and this link helps erect barriers to entry into the market for competitive provision of services. At the same time, competition between facilities themselves is less than it could be because of the link to services provision. The economics of services provision and the economics of facilities operations are different and one interferes with the other by imposing a restraining influence on competitive forces in both directions.

The industry organization suggested in this essay would allow quite intense competition among facilities to be the general rule. It would exist, as is already happening, among facilities that incorporate different technologies, such as wireline telephones and cellular telephones. However, the competition would not be between entire systems but between segments of different systems. For instance, cellular telephone operators need fixed-line trunks and switching between cellular base stations. Similarly, emerging PCS systems may need to piggyback on cellular base stations when PCS handsets are used in a moving vehicle. Telephone companies that want to deliver video dial tone would find it an advantage to be able to use the coaxial drops into homes owned by cable television operators. All cases of alternative technologies show that to make competition work there is no need for these technologies to be embodied in completely self-contained, stand-alone infrastructure. It is sufficient that they compete over only some segments of the total infrastructure network. This is because interconnection and interoperability allow a given technology to make its contribution to the network only in the most appropriate segment.

What is true and is seen to be beneficial in the case of alternate technologies is just as true and just as beneficial when it comes to competition among facilities incorporating identical technologies. For instance, trunk-line facilities between Canada's major cities can be duplicated (and have been) by different service providers. Service providers under the existing system had their reasons for "overbuilding" basic infrastructure since it has been the only way for some of them to get access to the extra profit margins that accrue from the presently imperfect competitive market for facilities. However, in a less imperfect world, where services provision and facilities provision are segregated, there are circumstances where the duplication of technology facilities would be equally justified.

Consider, for example, a case where the volume of use was high enough to justify building a second link, say, between two cities. Similarly, where the operator of an existing facility was earning abnormally high profits or where there was an unusually high degree of inefficiency in its operations, an alternative operator might then be able to build a duplicate facility and operate it at a profit, while still undercutting the price of the original operator. For this to be possible, the infrastructure has to be divisible into as many separate components as possible so that the efficiency test reflected by the price charged in each segment, compared with the price that a new entrant would charge for a parallel segment, is met everywhere along the network. Of course, any new provider of a particular segment must be able to interconnect with and interoperate within that segment *vis-à-vis* the rest of the network. The dual principle of interconnectivity and inter-operability, frequently implying a mandated open-network architecture, was recognized by the CRTC in its landmark decision of September 16, 1994 (decision 94-19). One requirement of the policy's implementation is the "unbundling" of both tariffs and the facilities themselves so as to create room for competitive entry. We will discuss in the following chapter the regulatory implications of such a regime for facilities operation. We can note here, however, that these implications are minimal. The most important is the need to monitor the performance of facilities operators with regard to compliance with the requirements of an open-network architecture, the compliance with common technical standards and the granting of non-discriminatory access both to other competitive operators of facilities and to intermediaries, that is to say service providers.

Economic Impact

If we are right about the best approach to take in order to make a successful transition to the environment created by the I-Way, then what are the economic implications?

With an industry structure where service providers (or, in our term, market intermediaries) are distinct from infrastructure operators, is there a risk that the sum of the resulting separate components is less than the sum of the previously integrated operations? In other words, are there economies of scope for broadcasters and telecommunications companies in providing both services and infrastructure? The frequency with which economies of scope are mentioned does not render the notion any less vague. The business administration literature in the 1980s was full of references to "synergy" in connection with the wave of mergers and acquisitions that washed over the whole economy of North America and to a lesser extent, Western Europe. "Economies of scope" and "synergy" are two different names for the same concept. Indications are that the concept is an empty one in most situations.

Possible exceptions arise when the businesses thought to be synergistic are in fact two different parts of the same business. In other words, economies of scope can mostly be found when the industries alleged to benefit from synergies have been mislabelled. There is obvious synergy between the manufacturing of right shoes and the manufacturing of left shoes, until you realize that we are talking about the same industry! By analogy, in the present context of the I-Way, one could say that broadcasting is the left shoe and telecommunications is the right shoe, since they are converging into one industry from both a technological and a regulatory perspective. However, that does not mean that we have to take it for granted that the broadcasting industry and telecommunications industries *as presently constituted* are the converging elements of an ultimately unified industry. The whole deck will be reshuffled, and this can happen in many ways. One way is through the law of the jungle of *laisser-faire* capitalism where, over a period of years, the winning combination will emerge as the survivor and the losing combination will simply have disappeared. This is likely to be what will happen in any case.

However, it is also possible for a broadcasting or telecom organization to anticipate the working out of these Darwinian forces and reorganize in such a way as to emerge with a winning formula. This is made easier if public policy can be similarly anticipatory.

If policy is to change to provide incentives and a context for evolution toward a model where infrastructure and service provision are distinct and at arm's length (let us call it the "two-tier model"), then a period of transition should be allowed for. In sectors that are as tightly regulated as broadcasting and telecommunications, roles cannot be altered from one day to the next without a lot of advance notification and an agreed-upon transition process. It would be outside the scope of the present essay to suggest what this process should be and how long the transition period should last. In choosing the speed of transition, there is most probably a tradeoff between the success of some and the survival of all.

The Focus of the I-Way: Economics Rather than Engineering

Most descriptions of the electronic I-Way are riddled with the vocabulary of the engineer: trunks, servers, local drops, nodes, signalling protocols, headends, starshape configuration and so on. This focus on engineering issues, challenges and breakthroughs is natural since it is engineering that provides the opportunity to even think about the I-Way. Accordingly, most graphical representations of the I-Way feature the carriage and switching networks as the star performers, very much at the centre of the picture, with customers and content providers on the periphery!

Such a focus, while understandable, is misleading and even dangerous if one is really interested in what will make the I-Way not just possible but successful. It is economics not engineering that must be seen to underlie the entire structure. It is this new system's ability to satisfy the end-user that will make the crucial difference. In that regard, current technical trials offered to a selected public at artificially low prices or at no cost have next to nothing to teach us. The viability of the I-Way will be tested over a long period of time when consumers have had occasion to experience it at realistic market prices and have decided whether or not it is worth their while. Judging from what has happened with other technologies, and allowing for the fact that the set of highway-related technologies includes some that have not yet been fully developed, we will have to wait until about 2010 to be able to judge the results.

However, that date – or for that matter any other – has no particular significance. What matters is whether or not the I-Way can prove itself economically and what it will really be like when it does. Technology by itself will not determine that. The content by itself will not play a particularly significant role either. As we have already indicated, the I-Way is not about content *per se* but about choice of content. It is about the ability of those who will offer the content and who will sift, edit, select, package, brand and enrich it that will determine whether the I-Way is cost effective or not. Apart from the interactive uses of the I-Way, all generic types of content that will travel the I-Way are generally available today in less expensive though perhaps less convenient ways.

In the accompanying two figures, an attempt is made to provide, in a much simplified way, a graphic representation of what the I-Way looks like both in its present divided state, with a quasi-watertight barrier between broadcasting and telecommunications, and what it could look like, according to the views expressed in this essay. Both figures are designed with the end-user in the central position and both have, at least in principle, a three-tier structure:

1. The first tier is made up of the end-user, equipped with end-user terminal equipment.

2. The second tier is the service provider tier, made up of the various businesses that provide services of all types to end-users.

3. The third tier is made up of all the input providers on the information I-Way, whether these inputs are content of various types or transfer infrastructure elements, systems and networks. Both content and infrastructure constitute the semi-finished goods, so to speak, that service providers use in various combinations and to which they add value in different measures to serve different end-user market segments.

figure 1

The *Status Quo* I-Way

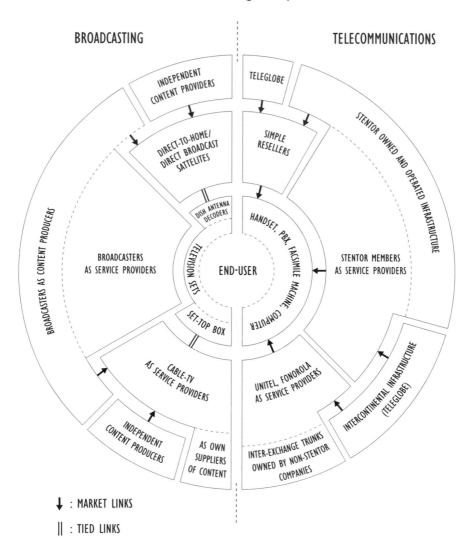

BROADCASTING

TELECOMMUNICATIONS

INDEPENDENT CONTENT PROVIDERS

TELEGLOBE

STENTOR OWNED AND OPERATED INFRASTRUCTURE

DIRECT-TO-HOME/ DIRECT BROADCAST SATTELITES

SIMPLE RESELLERS

DISH ANTENNA DECODERS

HANDSET, PBX, FACSIMILE MACHINE, COMPUTER

BROADCASTERS AS CONTENT PRODUCERS

BROADCASTERS AS SERVICE PROVIDERS

TELEVISION SETS

END-USER

STENTOR MEMBERS AS SERVICE PROVIDERS

SET-TOP BOX

CABLE-TV AS SERVICE PROVIDERS

UNITEL, FONOROLA AS SERVICE PROVIDERS

INTERCONTINENTAL INFRASTRUCTURE (TELEGLOBE)

INDEPENDENT CONTENT PRODUCERS

AS OWN SUPPLIERS OF CONTENT

INTER-EXCHANGE TRUNKS OWNED BY NON-STENTOR COMPANIES

↓ : MARKET LINKS

|| : TIED LINKS

figure 2

The Unified Three-Tiered I-Way

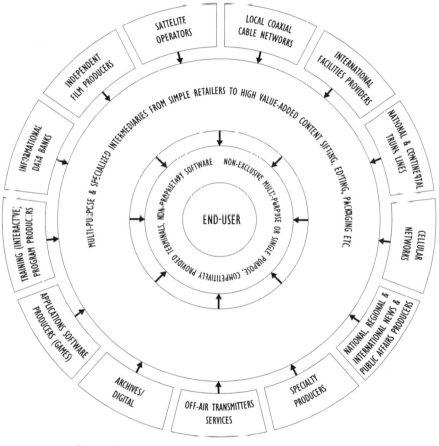

↓ : MARKET LINKS

Under our proposal (as reflected in figure 2), markets intervene between the tiers. Obviously, markets do not always exist under the *status quo,* as shown in figure 1. The most important service providers on either the broadcasting or the telecommunications side play the role of both intermediary and input provider. To that extent, a market that ought to exist has in its place a vertically integrated structure that limits competition and creates a barrier to entry.

End-users have access to equipment that is to some extent specific to one or other of the two sectors and, in the case of direct-to-home satellites and cable television, specific to one provider. Here again, this arrangement suppresses a market that should exist, and therefore limits choice and inhibits entry.

In figure 2, the middle tier would naturally be made up of thousands of small, medium and a few large firms offering intermediation services to a multitude of market segments. Would some of the present large players in broadcasting and telecommunications take their place among them? This is, of course, a choice they could make: however, one might expect the overwhelming majority to be new players rather than the established players of today. The difficulty confronting telephone companies, broadcasters and cable television companies is that they have grown and prospered under a regime that afforded them positions of power, due to their control of infrastructure. They have no tradition of listening to their consumers and responding to them in the way competitive firms do.

This middle tier is therefore essential to the success of the I-Way. It is the intermediary firms making up that tier that are crucial to the existence of the whole edifice. The market requires tremendous inventiveness and an open door to innovation and entrepreneurial talent. The other essential ingredient is a proper regulatory framework, an issue to which we now turn.

SEVEN

THE SERVICE VERSUS INFRASTRUCTURE DISTINCTION: HOW WOULD IT BE REGULATED?

Vastly expanded choice for both content and infrastructure is a distinguishing feature of the highway, compared to what used to obtain in both broadcasting and telecommunications. At the same time, immediacy, i.e., the elimination of distance as a factor, leads to a further expansion of choice on the I-Way. It would be tempting to argue, therefore, that the need to regulate will totally disappear. The ability to choose among alternative competitive suppliers would seem to put an end to the power of suppliers over users. Certainly with the old system of monopoly provision (a monopoly predetermined by the very nature of the facilities used) and with discretionary allocation of the electromagnetic spectrum (by definition a scarce input), regulatory intervention had to be front and centre. Monopoly power had to be checked and a scarce public resource had to be managed. But with the future I-Way in place, will there still be a need for regulation and, if so, what kind?

In this chapter, we do not raise again the issue of content regulation aimed at encouraging Canadian cultural production, except indirectly to point out where such an obligation would lie in the regulatory structure we recommend for the I-Way.

As well, we leave aside discussion of whether, in the intervening period before the I-Way is a full-fledged reality, existing regulations ought to be phased out, and at what pace. Attention is already being paid to this issue, most notably in the form of a shift, in country after country, away from regulating rates of return toward regulating prices and gradually liberalizing entry to the industry.

Common Carriage, Free Speech and Copyright

Telecommunications operate on the principle of common carriage. This means that the companies themselves are prohibited from interfering in any way with the content of the messages they carry. In return, they are protected against any attempt by third parties to hold them responsible for the content thus carried, whether obscene, politically objectionable, violent or related to criminal conspiracy. This mandated neutrality of common telecom carriers is in effect a guarantee of free speech, extended to electronic means of expression. Common carriage also entails non-discriminatory access to the network by anyone, at publicly posted prices. The advantage of this is not only that everyone pays the same price for the same length and type of service but also that transactions between users of telecommunications facilities and the company that operates them are simplified, since the conditions of use are known in advance and non-negotiable. This latter point is a great convenience if not an issue of high principle.

Common carriage is a very significant attribute in the context of this essay. We argue that any element of a telecommunications network should be available on an unbundled basis to any potential user, service provider or alternate operator of infrastructure without discrimination. This implies that all elements of infrastructure are interconnected and inter-operable. There is much in common between this concept and that of common carriage.

In contradistinction, broadcasting is based not on the principle of neutrality *vis-à-vis* content but on that of *responsibility* for content. Broadcasters are expected to produce content or acquire it from independent producers, integrate it into a schedule and obtain payment for it from advertisers or end-users. Government, at least in Canada, also expects broadcasters to shape content to fit public policy directions – for instance, to meet Canadian content rules under which an average 60 percent of television content must be of Canadian origin. While broadcasters are responsible for content, the law considerably restricts their legal liability *vis-à-vis* third parties because, in this country, the protection of free speech extends not only to the press but also to mass media by virtue of a specific reference to that effect in the Canadian Charter of Rights.[1]

Thus, while free speech is protected in both telecommunications and broadcasting, the way this is achieved varies and the beneficiaries of protection are quite different. In telecommunications, the ultimate beneficiary of free-speech protection is the end-user. In broadcasting, the beneficiary is the broadcaster itself rather than the end-user. As a result, the coming together of telecommunications and broadcasting on the I-Way raises the question of which regime should apply.

Even in the field of telecommunications, there are a number of elements that threaten the maintenance of common carriage principles (non-discriminatory access and non-interference with content). With the abolition of the monopoly features of telecommunications, any corporate entity can acquire or build a telecommunications infrastructure to serve its own private needs. It can also contract with established telecommunications carriers for the use of private-line facilities. As the name suggests, these private lines and networks are removed from the regime of common carriage. They become available to a client on the basis of a negotiated arrangement with the infrastructure operator or builder. Also, with increased commercial freedom to set rates for large business users on the basis of customized requirements (for instance AT&T tariff 12 in the US), the principle of non-discriminatory prices available to all according to a public-rate schedule is suffering from attrition. Professor Eli Noam contends that, in competition with common carriage, contract carriers are in a more favourable position and will slowly but surely doom common carriage to oblivion.[2] If this were to happen, the principle of non-interference with content in telecommunications would also be threatened. In an environment of expanded choice, contract carriers, like broadcasters, might very well see it to their advantage to censor content in response to clients' demands or in response to well-organized pressure groups.

The Charter of Rights does not protect society or minority views against self-censorship by broadcasters or by private carriers of telecommunications with no common carriage requirement. In a competitive environment, a particular broadcaster or carrier – or, in our term, an intermediary – that censors a particular content or message from a particular source could defend itself against accusations of contravening free-speech principles by pointing out that there are other intermediaries to which the source could turn.

As a result, the convergence of broadcasting and telecommunications – along with trends intrinsic to the telecommunications field such as the increasingly competitive environment in which it evolves and the spread of private services – may constitute a significant threat to a public, open, non-discriminatory I-Way.

Given the importance of Charter-based support for privacy protection, the significant and, it should be said, legitimate interest building in favour of adequate measures for copyright protection on the I-Way and, finally, concerns about obscene, violent and criminal use of the highway and the consequent call to minimize or repress such use, the prospect of having a viable liberal

I-Way consistent with the principles of a free and democratic society could easily be compromised. In sum, great care must be taken.

This suggests another reason why the distinction between services provision and infrastructure proposed in this essay is so important – namely, that it can help preserve a public, open, non-discriminatory communications network. The obligation to ensure access should rest with infrastructure providers: they should be responsible for providing an interconnected and inter-operable network capable of carrying any content, but without assuming control over, and therefore responsibility for, content.

The legal regime affecting service providers – intermediaries – would be totally different. The framework would by definition involve contractual links between intermediaries, content providers and infrastructure operators on the one hand, and end-users on the other. This regime would create for competitive intermediaries the following obligations:

- A legal responsibility for the content they offer with regard to the identity of the owner of the copyright, the adequacy of the licence held and the payment of royalties based either on a flat fee or on measured use gauged through the use of electronic turnstiles.

- Legal responsibility for the nature of the content, since by definition they would choose it, edit it, customize it, promote it and sell it to end-users. This liability for content would of course be balanced by the Charter's guarantee of freedom of expression for the media, which in turn would be qualified by restrictions imposed by public policy regarding, for example, the promotion of Canadian content or the suppression of violence and obscenity. The final balance would be struck by the courts as has been the case in the past.

- Legal responsibility *vis-à-vis* end-users but also *vis-à-vis* the public at large, under the heading of consumer protection. This includes protection of privacy since it would be through the access software and service offerings of intermediaries that data banks could be used and abused.

The responsibilities assigned to intermediaries may seem overwhelming. However, each of these must be present somewhere in the system. The I-Way cannot escape the rule of law; and these obligations are essential to an orderly and responsible use of a very powerful instrument. Our distinction between services provision and infrastructure provides an effective insulation for infrastructure operators, the backbone of the communications network, thus ensuring that the I-Way is turned into an instrument of democratization and expanded freedom and not an instrument of self-censorship and social control.

The Shifting Focus of Regulatory Activity

In the ideal system we envisage, the disappearance of statutory or otherwise officially sanctioned monopoly must be total. Construction of a segment of the wire portion of the I-Way infrastructure ought to be strictly a business decision (with the obligation of inter-operability and access), involving no need to seek approval in advance and with the market's view of financial viability being the only applicable criterion for decision making by the investors themselves. Needless to say, no one would be guaranteed a return, prices for the uses of the facilities would be set by the market and the chips would fall where they may. If any redundant facility was built, it would have to compete with existing infrastructure but it would also be subjected to the same requirements of inter-connection. It would have to be offered at a price competitive with that offered by similar infrastructure elements, in terms of technological improvement, higher reliability, enhanced quality etc.

Given the fixed-cost nature of infrastructure and the almost zero incremental cost related to its use, the market for infrastructure elements will tend to be one of capacity rather than usage. This is not unlike the competition that is taking place now between the facilities-based telephone companies and resellers. However, with the segregation of services provision from facilities operations, the entire market for infrastructure would be characterized by wholesale-type agreements, for which the only regulatory requirement is non-discriminatory access and pricing.

The wireless portion of the I-Way will still require licensing, as it must share a scarce natural resource, the electromagnetic spectrum. Such licensing should be based on principles of fairness and should ensure that competition in the sector – leading to complementary alternatives for service providers – is encouraged. Duplication and vertical integration of wireless infrastructure could create financial weaknesses and lead to bottlenecks that would be detrimental to both the service provider and the end-user. Licensing of this infrastructure will necessitate a balance between the different wire and wireless delivery systems. This balance, coupled with the principles of inter-operability and open access, will prevent the construction of a another infrastructure in an environment or a geographic area where the existing delivery system can produce equivalent service at lower price.

One must be aware that ensuring reciprocal access rights to infrastructure segments is a new development. As a principle, both the CRTC and the Government of Canada in its CRTC referral have endorsed it. Access rights are crucial to the avoidance of costly duplication and probably essential to ensuring the viability of a Canadian infrastructure. Implementation may, for all that, present some occasional difficulties. A particular infrastructure operator may resist allowing a competitor access to a key infrastructure element, arguing that all apparent "surplus" capacity is already spoken for. Could capacity be "reserved" for future use even by a third party? Would that entail a payment? These relatively technical points could in practice trump the principle. Rules and procedures need to be carefully laid down.

With no licence to award or review (except in the case of wireless transmission), no tariff to approve, no rate of return to assess on the basis of regulatory accounting requirements and no price cap to set, the business environment would shift from one where the regulator essentially second-guesses decisions made by the managers of operating companies to one where compliance in the new market of unbundled access and pricing, non-discriminatory treatment and open architecture needs to be monitored by every single market participant. The regulator's role became more one of a referee, acting on complaints. Non-discriminatory access for all would be enforced at the prodding of a complainant. In this sense, regulatory activity would shift from *a priori* authorization to a review of business practices made *a posteriori;* it would be focussed more on process and less on specific outcomes than is presently the case.

End-User Terminal Equipment

The need to create an open system that is fully competitive with regard to both infrastructure operations and services provision requires consideration of the end-user terminal equipment that the I-Way would use.

The regulatory requirements applying to such equipment are of particular importance. Historically, the first step usually taken to promote competition in telecommunications was to liberalize the provision of end-user terminal equipment. Telephone monopolies 25 years ago used to prohibit the use on their networks of equipment they had not themselves provided, typically through a rental arrangement with the end-user. The argument used most often was the need to maintain system integrity (i.e., a technical argument). The real reason, of course, was the additional income that could thus be earned without competitive challenge. Telephone handsets, PBX, fax machines, telephone answering systems *etc.* have been available in a competitive market in most countries for a few decades; the technical argument, therefore, is no longer heard. Telephone companies have lost control over this segment of the business and no longer think much about it. This is not true of the cable industry, where some video decoders and other set-top boxes are being developed or provided in a manner reminiscent of the situation of the telephone companies 30 years ago and not reflective of the present telecommunications picture.

There is much speculation about the nature of the end-user terminal equipment the I-Way will require. Most projections suppose a hybrid between a computer and a television set, although the precise shape of the hardware here is of secondary importance. What matters most is the access software; and, given the present regulatory vacuum on this issue, software companies are busy developing proprietary software, sometimes in strategic alliance with content producers or facilities operators.

The potential rewards for those who succeed in developing the best-performing access software are huge. This provides a tremendous incentive to inject the enormous sums needed for development work and therefore the *laisser-faire* environment is a great inducement to innovation. Experience shows that end-users are prepared to pay considerable sums to acquire terminal equipment that is specific to some types of content. Nintendo and Sega have each developed a succession of "consoles" that incorporate successive versions of software for their video games. One can suppose that the console market was profitable in and of itself; far more significant, however, is the fact that by buying a particular console, consumers are obliged to buy only compatible video game cassettes. Any content producer loves such a captive market, wherein even sales of compatible cassettes by independent producers generate income in the form of royalties.

The purchase price of eight-byte and 16-byte video-game consoles is relatively low, and the product is aimed at the notably affluent teenager market: as a consequence, the disadvantages of the formula are probably easy to dismiss. However, prices of end-user terminal equipment for the I-Way and the embodied access software will probably be sharply higher than those in the video game market. Terminal equipment now under development by some companies are a hybrid between a large high-definition television set and a personal computer, with a sophisticated coder/decoder, substantial memory, a printer and so on. The head of Time-Warner, which is running an experimental interactive television trial in Florida, complained that the set-top box developed for the purpose had a $5,000 price tag and a bulk more appropriate to a weight-lifting gymnasium than a living room!

The potential for creating captive markets should not be treated lightly. The very feasibility of competition in services provision, or what we have called the intermediary market for content and applications, crucially depends on the prohibition of such captive markets. While the prospects for success in the making and selling of such equipment and software to a worldwide public are huge, the commercial risks of failure are also of proportionate size. The VHS *vs.* Betamax battle comes to mind in this context. That example seems reassuring, as it suggests that proprietary technology is not the way to go – at least in the sense that using proprietary technology to build a quasi-monopoly may spell ultimate defeat even if the technology, in this case Betamax, is inherently superior. Far better would be to join proprietary technology with a business strategy that makes the technology universally available under licence: moreover, this approach seems more sensible from a public policy as well as a business perspective. It remains to be asked whether the precedents in this area provide sufficient reassurance to allow governments to leave the market to decide outcomes or whether compulsory licensing of access technologies should be imposed.

We grant that insufficient public debate has occurred to date on this issue. In part to stimulate such a debate, we suggest that compulsory licensing of access technology should indeed be imposed. This is very much in keeping with our other key recommendation – namely, making reciprocal access to infrastructure compulsory. Both proposals serve the objective of ensuring an open system. It is important to have competition at all levels not only for infrastructure segments, services and content provision but also for terminal equipment manufacture and sale.

Universal Services

Access to a telephone has emerged over the course of the 20th century as almost equivalent to a basic social right. While not enshrined in the constitution, universal access to basic service is no more contested, indeed even less contested, than some of the rights so enshrined.

With monopoly in the provision of telephone services persisting down to this day in many countries, the recognition of this right was a non-issue. The monopoly provider was expected, or if necessary compelled, to provide telephone service on a universal basis, with the associated costs reflected in the tariffs authorized by regulators. Universal service implied a subsidy that, it should be said, had little to do with the rate rebalancing issue taken as a whole. Rate rebalancing, in fact, had more to do with the evolving balance between the respective costs of local and long distance service and the consequent need to alter the tariffs set for each service. The cross subsidy at issue with regard to universal service refers to the difference in costs *within* the local service category between high-density service areas and lower-density ones; the subsidy also reflects demand-side considerations, irrespective of cost – for instance, the case of low-income users who can ill afford to pay standard charges for basic services.

Who should receive the subsidy for providing universal coverage in a world where there is competitive provision of basic telephone services? Further, to what extent is the segregation of services provision from facilities operations relevant to the issue of universal coverage?

With regard to the funding or, in other words, the source of financing for providing universal service, the tax-in-kind that used to be levied on the monopolist's rents must be replaced by a normal tax, payable in money by all end-users of I-Way services. For political reasons, one could expect that this tax might be levied on service providers, which would amount substantially to the same thing as taxing end-users, since service providers operating in a competitive environment would merely pass on the tax to the consumer. This is probably as it should be since, under such a system, those who can afford I-Way services will subsidize those who cannot or who live in remote areas where the cost of providing service is prohibitively high.

However, such a shift from an implicit tax levied on monopoly service providers to a normal explicit tax paid by all service providers does not entirely dispose of the issue. There remains the question of defining what is meant by "essential services" in the context of universal coverage. This question is rendered considerably more complicated by the emergence of the I-Way. The difficulty does not reside solely in the wide variety of broadband offerings that one could conceivably want to include in a definition of universal service. There is also the important issue of defining a minimum service. This was addressed in the past by simply maintaining a low monthly charge for connection to the telephone system under the normal practice of unlimited local usage. In the US, the question was raised anew when the US regulator allowed a very considerable increase in basic telephone monthly charges starting in 1984 for the purposes of rate rebalancing. (In Canada, the basic monthly charges for local telephone service remained almost constant during the period.) The rise in the basic monthly charge in the US threatened universality, and various options were developed with the goal of minimizing the subsidy requirements for maintaining universal access. By further refining what is meant by universal service, customers are now offered a choice among a large number of options, some of them with very low price tags indeed. Whatever the definition adopted in a world of multiple providers of services, a public bidding process for providing basic services at lowest cost looks like a promising approach.

Further refinement of what is meant by "public goods" on the I-Way seems to be leading toward a distinction between individual and collective usage. Assuming that the I-Way becomes an indispensable tool for professional qualification, retraining and regional development, it can be argued that access to the I-Way in remote locations or for economically disadvantaged people through public facilities such as schools, libraries and community centres, at least for the high-cost, high-bandwidth features, might constitute an adequate arrangement to ensure universal access. Whether the access is individual or collective, competitive provision of the subsidized services seems to be a logical corollary to the structure envisaged in this essay.

Once a decision has been made about the desired scope of subsidized services (from basic to enhanced, from individual to collective) and bids are received from intermediaries, the resulting infrastructure extensions could be built and services provided in the same way as they are for self-supporting offerings: no specific infrastructure operator or intermediary would be under any other obligation.

The Question of Structural Separation

What exactly is implied by the suggestion in this paper that the provision of services on the I-Way ought to be distinguished from the business of providing the infrastructure? At present, the confusion of roles is so complete that to most people the suggestion that two different businesses are involved sounds strange and fanciful. Changing this would obviously require very substantial effort.

There is a continuum of alternative options between the *status quo,* under which only fully integrated infrastructure-cum-retail services firms operate, and the opposite extreme, under which fully divested, independently managed and owned corporate entities operate either the infrastructure or the retail business but not both.[3]

An example of an extreme form of separation, namely divestiture, can be seen in the results of the US decision on January 1, 1984 to split up the previously fully integrated telephone company AT&T, resulting in the formation of a long-distance and international telecommunications company, AT&T itself, and seven regional Bell operating companies, restricted to local communications.

CABLE & WIRELESS

Jonathan Solomon MA
Executive Director, Strategy and
Corporate Business Development

As requested, a copy

In between the two extremes, one can identify the following possibilities:

- closest to the *status quo,* the introduction of separate accounting, whereby ownership, control and management are common but the respective costs of the two businesses are calculated separately;

- organizational separation, where ownership and control remain common but management is split up along the two broadly defined lines of business;

- structural separation where management and control are exercised separately but ownership alone remains common.

Which option is the best? The answer, whatever it is, will remain hotly debated. Surely the only guide in making the choice resides in determining the objectives that are to be served by organizational reform. The objectives are clearly public in nature and therefore implementation probably implies a formal statutory requirement. Complete segregation of infrastructure from service provision is not ever likely to be willingly chosen by a telecommunications or any I-Way corporate entity. It represents the loss of a very significant degree of freedom for the firm – a loss, that is, of the infrastructure or monopoly revenue that can help it win the battle in more competitive markets. Who would willingly give that up?

It is interesting that regulators in Australia, the United Kingdom and, now, Canada have all adopted the milder form of separation, namely separate accounting. This presumably reflects the judgement that accounting separation is in some sense the least costly option. It also at least implicitly represents acceptance of some of the arguments against more radical forms of separation.

The first of these arguments usually consists of the assertion that, with more radical separation and certainly with divestiture, both the company and its clients lose the benefits of "economies of scope" – in other words, "synergy" between infrastructure and services. Unless this assertion refers to the ability to cross-subsidize one with the other, something which any form of separation is designed to prevent, these general references to economies of scope are never well documented and, as we argued earlier, easy to dismiss.

A serious argument resides in the American experience with AT&T's divestiture, a step that some analysts now believe was ill-founded and is likely soon to be reversed, if only because AT&T is bound sooner or later to become an active participant in local telecommunications. However, this point can be conceded without supporting the notion that divestiture was wrong. In the 10 years since divestiture, there has been a powerful stimulus to greater competition in long distance services. It is this competition that has, in turn, prompted AT&T's re-entry into local services through alternative technologies such as cellular telephony.

There are fundamental reasons why separate accounting is insufficient as a basis for a genuine functional distinction between lines of businesses. One is that it appears very difficult to develop and use a method of cost allocation under a regime of separate accounting that is, at the same time, not unreasonably complicated and not contentious. Cost allocation in an industry characterized by high fixed costs contains many arbitrary elements that will provoke a steady supply of arguments from people who dislike the consequences flowing from the application of any particular method. Canada, following CRTC decision 94-19, has now embarked on the separate accounting path and has already begun to experience difficulty in reaching consensus. This debate is just an extended and broader version of the ongoing debate about contributions made by competitors to Stentor's network to make up the deficiency in the local services account.

However, even more telling than arguments about implementation difficulties is the fact that, under any regime short of complete structural separation, the change in corporate culture required to transform a former monopolist operator of telecommunications infrastructure into a competitively minded provider of content and retail services may not be possible. Any formula that preserves common management is likely to leave in place for some time the traditional corporate culture associated with infrastructure facilities operators. This, it might be said, is by nature a transitional difficulty and an obstacle that with time might be overcome.

However, what can never be overcome are the necessary implications of a system of separate accounting – namely, total disclosure of information with regard not only to the operation of the infrastructure but to the whole business. There seems to be an inherent contradiction between fostering a competitive industry for services and imposing the regulatory requirement that the accounts, cost breakdowns and profitability by activity of the most significant competitor in the services business – that is to say the company that formerly was involved in providing not only services but the infrastructure itself – should be open to public scrutiny and therefore to competitors as well.

Notes

1. Eli M. Noam, "Beyond Liberalization – From the Network of Networks to the System of Systems," *Telecommunications Policy,* Vol. 18, no. 4 (May 1994), pp. 286-94; Eli M. Noam, "Beyond Liberalization II, The Impending Doom of Common Carriage," *Telecommunications Policy,* Vol. 18, no. 6 (July 1994), pp. 435-52.

2. The Honourable Justice John Sopinka, "Freedom of Speech and Privacy in the Information Age," an address presented at the University of Waterloo Symposium on Free Speech and Privacy in the Information Age, November 26, 1994, mimeo.

3. Martin Cave and Ian Martin, "The Cost and Benefits of Accounting Separation" (The Australian and British debates), *Telecommunications Policy,* Vol. 18, no. 1 (January-February 1994), pp. 12-20; "Interconnection and Accounting Separation," Consultative Document, Issued by the Director General of Telecommunications, Oftel Office of Telecommunications, London, England, June 1993, pp. 1-13; Arthur Andersen, "Interconnection and Accounting Separation," Response to Consultative Document (mimeo).

EIGHT

INTERNATIONAL DIMENSIONS

This essay has been written from a Canadian perspective. There are several references to Canada and to Canadian content. There is also some mention of a "small-country perspective" which most readers will recognize as yet another reference to Canada's self-perception *vis-à-vis* its neighbour to the south, the United States. However, there is nothing in the concerns that are reflected in this essay that make them inherently irrelevant to any other country, even the US.

The I-Way is hailed for making the world smaller. It is celebrated for making possible the sharing, on a worldwide basis and instantaneously, the entire world's wealth of points of view, experiences and creativity. It therefore has an inescapable international dimension.

The potential for the new technology of the I-Way to change our civilization irrevocably makes it worthwhile to consider the implications of the whole concept as a basis for international action, in trade terms particularly. Its importance as a domestic policy issue is what underpinned much of the preceding chapters. Our point here is that the I-Way's potential must also inspire action and agreements to deal with the international dimensions of the highway. Information, whether under its traditional labels of broadcasting or telecommunications, has such an impact on the way we live that it cannot simply be treated as just another industry when it comes to international treaty obligations.

Among the reasons why the US is sometimes regarded as a threat when it comes to the I-Way, apart from the sheer size of its domestic market and the dominant influence in the world of its entertainment industry, is the remarkable tendency of US discussions about the I-Way to generate, at least in the minds of foreign observers, the impression that issues of quality and richness of life along the I-Way are somehow an improper topic of discussion: merely so much quasi-philosophical speculation about which no one can prove anything let alone come to an agreement. Even if some consensus could be reached about how to go about developing the I-Way, the combined forces of technology and economics are in any case so strong that they will determine the outcome irrespective of any such consensus. Finally, to cap it all, there is a belief that with or without consensus, governments are powerless to act in any meaningful way, not only because of the inherent difficulty of shaping the blind forces of economics and technology, but beyond that because of the particular frailty of governments, their timidity in appealing to the public interest over and above the pushing and shoving of opposing domestic interests and the lack of attention paid by the general public to policy issues.

These nihilistic feelings are particularly strong in the US, and are even being raised by some academics to the level of a theory of government. However, they are also strongly at variance with the concerns expressed by Europeans about the same topic. This nihilism and the reactions it provokes are also a factor in many countries' desire to manage the I-Way in such a way as to maintain their distinct cultural identities, values and outlook on life.

In this chapter, we will consider two questions. The first is the extent to which a non-dominant country can independently and so to speak unilaterally enforce the vision of an open system for the highway – open at least in the sense that its segment of the global information highway would allow that country to be and remain an active participant and find a voice for itself and its own culture. The second question is the apparently easier one of how to achieve the same purpose in the context of a multilateral web of mutual obligations and safeguards.

The Unilateral Approach

What are the prospects of maximizing the advantages of the highway for a non-dominant country acting on its own? We will focus here on just a few salient issues. To fix ideas more concretely, here as in preceding chapters, issues are discussed from a Canadian perspective.

It is not generally understood in Canada that economies of scale for highway infrastructure are such that a significant part of Canada could be served by using US infrastructure at very close to zero marginal cost. This means that the cost involved in using infrastructure would be minimized if Canada were to be considered a simple adjunct to the continental US, at least in cases where massive trunks and switching capacity are appropriate. Of course, this could be a very advantageous outcome for Canadians since they would enjoy a higher standard of living if they could thereby save much of the resources that they would otherwise have to use to build and maintain their own infrastructure. This is true for the same reason that unilateral tariff reduction is advantageous.

However, there is no assurance that the prices that Canadians would have to pay for using US infrastructure would reflect the very low costs made possible by economies of scale. The Canadian market is very small relative to the US market and there is therefore no guarantee that competition would be as intense in Canada as it would be in the US. Indeed, it could be argued that if American infrastructure operators failed to sufficiently lower their prices for services provided in Canada, Canadian competitors might emerge; however, even then, they could easily be discouraged by the knowledge that US firms enjoyed large margins that could be slashed if Canadian firms were to enter the market. Further, even if US facilities operators dropped their prices in Canada to a very low level, they could be expected to engage in substantial cream-skimming of the small Canadian market, taking large business customers for themselves and leaving other segments of the market to Canadian operators, making it even harder for these Canadian companies to enjoy economies of scale and provide services at advantageous prices. In such a situation, the only unilateral response that a Canadian government could adopt would be to levy high taxes on those market segments enjoying lower made-in-the-US prices so as to, in some way or other, subsidize the other, non-competitive, segments of the market. The overall results might not be to save Canada any money but the distribution of the costs would be different.

There is another possible response to the threat represented by disproportionate economies of scale available to US facilities operators. This consists in applying to US firms the mandate imposed on facilities operators in Canada to use Canadian facilities. However, it is difficult, from a technological point of view, to monitor compliance with such a requirement. This difficulty, always present irrespective of industry structure, becomes more acute the more competitive the telecommunications industry becomes.

As a general principle, radical unbundling of businesses and infrastructure elements with full interconnection rights and an open architecture is the policy most likely to favour domestic enterprises whose small scale would otherwise be a handicap. Economies of scale for facilities do not apply everywhere, and are in some cases offset by disadvantages incurred by large organizations. A general prohibition against integrated industrial structures, an accompanying requirement that integrated foreign players enter Canada in only one capacity and the enforcement of arm's length relations with the rest of the enterprise together offer the best unilateral response to a non-dominant country and help it keep the door open for the involvement of its own nationals in, if not all aspects of the highway, at least a significant number of segments.

Bilateral and Multilateral Options

For a non-dominant country that wants to maintain an open environment for the I-Way, bilateral or preferably multilateral options offer intriguing possibilities. However, to make these possibilities real, the nature of multilateral undertakings contracted under trade agreements must reflect in a creative fashion the features that are special to telecommunications or, more generally, to the creation of genuine freedom of trade with regard to services, a policy area that is still relatively new.

The single most significant advantage of a multilateral option is to make economies of scale potentially available to all enterprises, whatever their country of first incorporation. This is equally the case with regard to facilities, content production and intermediation. A larger market is advantageous for all players, even those from a dominant country, since it permits all to fully exploit economies of scale. Given that firms from a dominant country are, at least initially, already further along their decreasing cost curves, they enjoy a large early advantage that should probably be offset for a time through adequately devised transitional safeguards. Ultimately, market expansion makes it unnecessary to retain safeguards on the use of facilities by the smaller players. However, the need for special financing for network development in underserved areas or for the maintenance of basic services for remote communities and lower-income end-users remains and is perhaps even more acute. A fiscal-type levy is therefore probably inevitable and fund allocations from the resulting pool may become a contentious issue among signatories to a multilateral agreement.

It might be expected that, with the resulting increase in efficiency all around, this issue could be resolved painlessly, with everyone being left better off as a result. It might be hoped that such a unified I-Way market created by contracting parties could fully develop within a unified legal and regulatory I-Way environment, at least to the point of allowing for a "common passport." This expression, borrowed from the European Union's single market approach, implies either exemptions from licensing procedures for firms active on the I-Way and incorporated and controlled from within one of the signatory countries or the automatic granting of national licences to any such firm.

A more difficult issue is the need for harmonized rules with regard to industry structure. This essay has made plain the advantages of enforcing generally open access for all content providers, facilities operators and intermediaries, in order to maintain an open highway and help it achieve its promise of genuine diversity. If an international agreement on highway-related services did not cover industry structure and business practices, national regulations governing such issues might well vary in ways that could effectively restrict choice, restrain access and limit competition. For instance, American industrial policy might take a lenient view of vertical integration, allowing very large firms to behave in a self-sufficient manner in terms of both content production and facilities use. Such practices might effectively nullify a significant part of the gain from a nominally open common market for I-Way inputs.

Somewhat ironically, this problem is similar to the one faced by the Americans themselves with regard to their firms' entry into Japanese markets. Negotiations over so-called "structural impediments" between the two countries have been going on for years with little progress. The Americans are concerned that the structures, in particular, of the flat glass and automobile industries in Japan are such that, as a result of exclusive distribution agreements between Japanese distributors and manufacturers, foreign producers of either good are effectively shut out of the market. The need to set up an entirely separate distribution infrastructure for US imports into Japan makes market entry impractical, even though tariffs and quotas, the traditional trade impediments, are no longer an issue. The Americans, after long thought, have suggested remedies that might well prove applicable in a contemplated integration of the North American I-Way markets.

In the case of telecommunications and broadcasting, the major two constituent parts of the I-Way, there is an additional reason for policy harmonization. These sectors are, in all countries, regulated industries. As a consequence, industry structure, business practice and regulations are closely intertwined. No government can pretend to wash its hands of how businesses in these fields behave, even in the absence of state ownership of the firms in question.

Finally, assuming a measure of harmonization of regulatory practices, at least to the extent of establishing certain common objectives for regulatory intervention, there is the problem of enforcement. What happens if the rules are breached? What happens in particular if a commitment to the effect that a firm from country A should have access to country B is somehow ignored or frustrated? This point is related to the preceding one in the sense that breaches of treaty commitments are more likely to find their origin in business practices than in state action or inaction. Sales of services that are lost today cannot be recouped by the sale of the same services tomorrow, as is sometimes possible in the case of merchandise trade. To be effective, relief for this type of problem can only be injunctive, coupled with a right to compensation, payable to the aggrieved party by the offending party. The simplified procedure of joint panels with powers to bind the parties might constitute the best venue to enforce treaty commitments and apply statutory sanctions.

From an historical perspective, the advent of the I-Way is just the last in a long series of momentous developments that have similarly shrunk the world by enabling people to visit each other, to exchange goods and ideas and to know more about each other: these include offshore navigation, the printing press, steam power, the telegraph and air travel. In this ladder toward greater universality of human experience, toward the "global village," the I-Way is a high step for humanity to climb. It is more complex but also more far-reaching than anything that has gone on before.

The coming to maturity of the I-Way means excitement for a few, prosperity for some and, one hopes, a higher level of civilization for all. Everything suggests that the technological aspects of the I-Way will be ready before we are as human beings. As usual, human beings will have to adapt and in this, a little forethought would help.

Shrinking the planet, getting all of us to live, so to speak, more closely together, implies cultivating a greater degree of mutual respect. As human experience has shown, the only rational response to closer physical or intellectual propinquity is to cultivate a better understanding of the fact that such propinquity is a two-way process. As the world shrinks and we get to live more closely together, no one can expect to be doing all the talking and no one can expect that self-restraint is only for others. It is an interesting thought that one of the features of the I-Way is its interactive capability. If it is truly interactive, it may spell the end of a monopoly for top-down structures, and the dawn of a more democratic, interactive dialogue where the top-down flow is counterbalanced by a flow in the opposite direction.

change affects a myriad of things in ways that, because they make no head-lines, are generally unknown by the general public: new industrial processes, new materials, new management methods, new merchandising channels and so on. Moreover, the innovations that do reach headline proportions, such as the microprocessor and fibre optics, only constitute the tip of the iceberg. It has become trivial to describe these changes and, in addition, to suggest that more are on the way. The mapping of the human genome and breakthroughs in molecular biology promise to open yet more new frontiers.

The link between scientific and technological developments and social and economic change is both direct and indirect. The indirect link goes through trade liberalization and globalization, which themselves reflect the new corporate realities made possible by computers and telecommunications. A very significant portion of total international trade, and an even greater proportion of its growth in the past 20 years, reflects the rise of the transnational corporation: much international trade takes place between branches of the same TNC, situated in different countries around the globe. Such corporations would not exist nearly in the same numbers, nor embody principles of an international division of labour to the same extent, were it not for technological advances in transportation and telecommunications.

The notion that more technological change is on its way is firmly rooted in a worldwide and massive research and development effort. For about half a century now, research and development have become institutionalized. The lone researcher or pioneer inventor working in his basement still exists but they are no longer what drives scientific research and technological innovation. There is now a huge research and development establishment, not any longer just in half a dozen countries but in scores of countries around the world. R&D has acquired its vested interests lobbies and is everywhere economically and politically well entrenched. What is perhaps most significant is that R&D has come to be seen as a way to make money and not only, as it used to be seen, as a way to spend it. Floating new ideas, new products and new technologies has become popular with investors and rewarding for promoters.

Beyond the glitzy image of progress, there is, therefore, an implied message: change is everywhere, change is more rapid than our ability to adjust to it, more change is inexorably coming our way and, finally, change is sudden and unpredictable. This implied message is far from encouraging; on the contrary, it is disabling, disorienting and leads easily to a form of political paralysis. The suggestion is: do not delude yourselves into thinking that change can be purposeful rather than random, that change can be steered, that change can be anticipated and therefore that one can prepare oneself for it as opposed to merely, *a posteriori,* adapting to it. Indeed, the often-heard injunction about the need to adapt sounds almost like a confession of failure.

In this essay, we have tried to indicate that the direction of change is not so mysterious and that it can be anticipated at least in rough outlines. We also pointed out that change can be shown to be not so rapid after all since it depends not only on what is technologically feasible but also on the rate at which people can absorb new technology. Finally, we have tried to suggest ways in which this country ought to prepare itself, while there is time, for the coming changes and simultaneously influence the direction of change. Canada is already well advanced in this. However, the I-Way requires an extra push. This essay is an attempt to suggest where that extra push should lead us.

There are four principal points that we have tried to get across:

1. Mandated segregation of infrastructure operations or content production from the intermediary function. The need here is to make room for markets between intermediaries and providers of content, applications software and telecommunications facilities in lieu of allowing full sway to the vertically integrated firm with its predetermined relationships and relatively closed, self-contained philosophy. This segregation should take the form of enforced structural separation, at a minimum, and be implemented over a reasonable transition period of, say, five years. It would, in various sub-sectors of the I-Way, have the following implications:

   • for telephone companies, a clear partition of the existing businesses between infrastructure operations and services provision;

   • for cable television companies, a separation between their dual roles as infrastructure providers and as broadcasters responsible for selecting, packaging and marketing content;

   • for broadcasters themselves, including the CBC, a decision to focus more clearly on content generation; and finally,

   • for film exhibitors, a prohibition against their being owned and controlled by film-makers.

2. Mandated interconnection and inter-operability for all infrastructure operators and uninhibited reciprocal access down to single elements of

infrastructure, with the accompanying liberalization of the regulatory regime to limit licensing to wireless only, thereby opening up the field to full competitive provision. Licensing of wireless at the infrastructure level, although not at the service level, should prevent vertical integration and duplication, all the while ensuring fair and sustainable competition.

3. A strategic shift in Canadian cultural policy away from protectionism and toward export-oriented policies and business strategies. Official incentives could still exist but on a targeted basis only, to support commercial strategies and, if indeed required, non-exportable nation-building content.

4. Systematic efforts to obtain concurrence on these objectives from other countries and support for their implementation through appropriate treaty commitments.

These suggestions, if implemented, would lead to major changes and require adjustments in our current telecommunications and broadcasting industries. The process selected by the government to encourage discussion and study of these and similar recommendations must allow every participant within the industry the time and opportunity to react, measure the consequences and contribute to the debate. Our goal in writing this essay was simple: to provide a direction for Canada in its efforts to position itself as one of the leaders of the information society throughout the world.

RECENT IRPP PUBLICATIONS

CITY-REGIONS

Andrew Sancton, *Governing Canada's City-Regions: Adapting Form to Function*
William Coffey, *The Evolution of Canada's Metropolitan Economies*

EDUCATION

Bruce Wilkinson, *Educational Choice: Necessary But Not Sufficient*
Peter Coleman, *Learning About Schools: What Parents Need to Know and How They Can Find Out*
Edwin G. West, *Ending the Squeeze on Universities*

GOVERNANCE

Donald G. Lenihan, Gordon Robertson, Roger Tassé, *Canada: Reclaiming the Middle Ground*
F. Leslie Seidle (ed.), *Seeking a New Canadian Partnership: Asymmetrical and Confederal Options*
F. Leslie Seidle (ed.), *Equity and Community: The Charter, Interest Advocacy and Representation*
F. Leslie Seidle (ed.), *Rethinking Government: Reform or Reinvention?*

PUBLIC FINANCE

Paul A.R. Hobson and France St-Hilaire, *Toward Sustainable Federalism: Reforming Federal-Provincial Fiscal Arrangements*

SOCIAL POLICY

Ross Finnie, *Child Support: The Guideline Options*
Elisabeth B. Reynolds (ed.), *Income Security: Changing Needs, Changing Means*
Jean-Michel Cousineau, *La Pauvreté et l'État: Pour un nouveau partage des compétences en matière de sécurité sociale*

CHOICES/CHOIX

Social Security Reform:
IRPP prend position / The IRPP Position
Commentaries on the Axworthy Green Paper

THESE AND OTHER PUBLICATIONS ARE AVAILABLE FROM

Renouf Publishing
1294 Algoma Road
Ottawa, Ontario
K1B 3W8

Tel.: (613) 741-4333
Fax.: (613) 741-5439